SAGE CONTEMPORARY SOCIAL SCIENCE ISSUES 47

THE LIBRARY
SIMON'S ROCK EARLY COLLEGE
ALFORD ROAD
GREAT BARRINGTON, MA 01230

CONVERSION CAREERS

In and Out of the New Religions

Edited by

James T. Richardson

 SAGE PUBLICATIONS   *Beverly Hills / London* 1978

821594 BL 53 .R5x

The material in this publication originally appeared as a special issue of
AMERICAN BEHAVIORAL SCIENTIST (Volume 20, Number 6, July/
August 1977). The Publisher would like to acknowledge the assistance of the
special issue editor, James T. Richardson.

Copyright © 1977 by Sage Publications, Inc. This edition first published
Fall 1978.

**All rights reserved. No part of this book may be reproduced or utilized in any
form or by any means, electronic or mechanical, including photocopying,
recording, or by any information storage and retrieval system, without
permission in writing from the publisher.**

For information address:

SAGE Publications, Inc.
275 South Beverly Drive
Beverly Hills, California 90212

SAGE Publications Ltd
28 Banner Street
London EC1Y 8QE

Printed in the United States of America
International Standard Book Number 0-8039-1025-8
Library of Congress Catalog Card Number 77-95434

SECOND PRINTING

CONTENTS

Conversion Careers

In and out of the New Religions

In recent years many new and different types of religious groups have developed both here and abroad, attracting for various lengths of time hundreds of thousands of participants. These new groups have stood out against the allegedly darkening sky of growing secularism like a fireworks display on a Fourth of July evening. A population defined by many as "too sophisticated for religion" has responded with astonishment to the resurgence of interest in things religious. And sometimes the astonishment has changed quickly to anger and frustration when media accounts (verified or not) about the beliefs and practices of some of the new groups were presented.

This interdisciplinary collection of papers, developed around the topic of "conversion and commitment in contemporary religion," is part of a broad effort to understand all the social movements and groups that have been a part of the chaotic social scene during the past decade or so. Thus, the collection can be viewed as a contribution to the literature on social movements, as well as a specific contribution to the scientific study of religion. The papers in this issue are pitched at what might be termed the social-psychological level of analysis. This kind of analysis attends to the individual in relationship to the group, and seems the logical way to approach any discussion of conversion and commitment. Conversion is usually thought of as happening to individuals, and there is some appreciation among social and behavioral scientists that conversion usually occurs as a result of certain kinds of interactions with others, who are usually members of some group. Further, there is an understanding that, in most instances, commitment grows within a group context.

This more social-psychological approach is, of course, but one way to view the current situation. For instance, when one talks of conversion to a movement or movement group, ipso facto one is also talking about how a movement or group starts and gains and keeps recruits, so that it may last over time. Allusion should be made to societal level conditions that "furnish" potential recruits. Attention must also be given to the organizational aspects of recruitment, and some information about the individual characteristics of potential converts and converts needs to be available.

Studying conversion and commitment in contemporary religion at a social-psychological level is important for reasons other than the idiosyncratic interest of some social and behavioral scientists. Much concern has been generated about recruitment tactics allegedly used by some of the new religious groups and movements, and this concern has been made manifest in the media through charges of "brainwashing," kidnapping, and the use of other forms of coercion by some groups. Governmental authorities at every level have had to deal with this issue. Thus, we find that the general public is not so concerned about societal conditions that led to the new movements, or to the characteristics of individuals who join. Instead, attention at the popular level has focused on the organization of recruitment efforts by the new groups. This is understandable from the human point of view, for parents and friends of the thousands of converts to the new movements are genuinely concerned about the welfare of converts, and are puzzled and alarmed at their affiliation with new and strange groups. The widespread concern, even hysteria, on the part of so many might also be viewed fruitfully as a predictable form of displacement, scapegoating, or an ingenious use of the "outside agitator" theory to explain away extant problems. Whatever the reason, it is plain that much lay interest has focused on recruitment methods. Scholarly interest has grown as well, as indicated by this issue and other recent work.

A dramatic way of demonstrating the popular concern about recruitment methods of some new religious groups is given by the decision to include a paper on the reaction to the new movements embodied in the so-called "deprogramming movement." The paper by Shupe, Spielmann, and Stigall serves as an ironic capstone to this issue devoted to the topic of conversion and commitment in contemporary religion. The authors have been involved in an important study of the burgeoning anticult movement, a movement which is just as obviously in the "conversion business" as any of the new religious groups and movements. Deprogramming, which is at least a form of rigorous resocialization, has attracted international attention, and is being dealt with in many forums. The courts are deciding whether or not kidnapping is a part of the process, as well as being the scene of some recent pitched legal battles over the creative use of conservatorship laws being attempted by some segments of the anticult movement.

The ACLU is involved with this issue, as are other lay and scholarly groups, along with many individual people, on either side of the issue. Much hinges on the outcome of this considerable attention being focused on new religious movements and their "reactions," an attention totally unpredictable just a few years ago, when we were nearly all in agreement that the "age of secularization" had arrived, and that we, as a society, were getting too politically conscious to be interested in religion of any kind. Who would have guessed that freedom of religion would be a major issue in the news in the mid-1970s?

COMMENTS ON CONCEPTUALIZATION AND METHODS

Several different methodologies have been used in the research reported in this issue. This adds to the strength of the collection in that it offers something for most readers and it affords some cross-checking for validity. Much of the work described has been done using the participant-observer approach, but other research techniques also have been used, including personality assessment, content analysis of documents, interviewing, and survey research. Some will not care for the fact that there is little statistical analysis exhibited in the papers (see Heirich, 1977, for a good example of using such techniques in this area of study). Others will respond to the integration of methods used and to the considerable attention given in some papers to the actual statements of members of the groups (see Taylor, 1976, for a defense of such a humanistic approach). Suffice it to say that the papers were not selected for this collection because of the use of certain research techniques. Instead, they were chosen because they seemed to contain important and valid information and analysis about the topic of interest.

Nowhere in this introduction or in any of the papers is there a thorough conceptual analysis of the terms conversion and commitment. A decision was made to include as many papers as possible illustrating how scholars use the terms in their research (if only implicitly), instead of using space to specify certain definitions of such key terms. In part, the decision was prompted by the availability of so many solid papers, but also there was recognition of the basic futility of trying to delineate terms that have so many uses, in both the scholarly and lay literature. If readers are particularly interested in the meaning of such terms, they might examine such varied sources as Travisano (1970), Gordon (1974), Richardson (1977), Kiesler (1971), and Zygmunt (1972).

There is obviously a large literature that relates to the basic concepts of conversion and commitment, and those just listed are but a sample, and a limited one at that. As indicated earlier, the thrust of this set of papers is social-psychological, and, thus, much of social psychology relates to what is being studied in these papers. In one sense this collection of papers can be seen as evidence for Liska's (1977: 2) claim that social psychology has "dissipated" into a variety of subfields of sociology. This collection of papers and other work derived from the study of contemporary religious movements suggests that the social-psychological study of conversion and commitment is indeed being pursued more in the sociology and psychology of religion than anywhere else at this time. However, much relevant literature on the basic processes involved is being produced in other subfields. For instance, studies of socialization, resocialization, "disaffection," rehabilitation, social movement growth and change, occupational changes, attitude change, and behavior modification and control all may be relevant, and may well offer important take-off points for future research on religious conversion and commitment. For instance, much research on religious conversion focuses on changes in belief systems, whereas some of the areas just listed focus on behavioral changes. The integration of findings from both perspectives would seem to be useful (see Kiesler, 1971, for a provocative attempt at relating cognitive and behavioral elements).

CONCLUDING COMMENT

Conspicuous by their absence are papers dealing directly with conversion and commitment to more traditional religious groups. Certainly, attention could have been more obviously paid to the phenomena of increased growth of certain kinds of churches and problems of lack of growth in other churches (see Kelly, 1972, and Bibby and Brinkerhoff, 1974, for relevant discussions). The Westley paper on the Charismatic Renewal movement in the Catholic church comes nearest to a study of conversion and commitment in traditional religion. However, several of the other papers relate indirectly to traditional religion, both Eastern and Western, in ways that will be clearer after reading the selections. For instance, one reason for the continued growth of some more conservative churches in America is the simple fact that they have tapped new religious phenomena such as the Jesus movement. Not unexpectedly, many youth who convert to the Jesus movement end up in conservative and Pentecostal churches, or the groups to which they belong become a part of "established" religion. Also, converts to some new groups as described herein come from more traditional religious groups. They are attracted to these new groups in part apparently because of the relative lack of excitement and meaning they found in traditional churches. The rapid establishment of ties between new religious groups and traditional religious institutions means that (1) many people will flow from one to the other, and that (2) traditional religion may well be changing itself in the direction of some of the new movements. Thus, we feel comfortable in presenting this selection of papers under the topic of "Conversion and Commitment in Contemporary Religion."

—James T. Richardson
University of Nevada, Reno

REFERENCES

BIBBY, R. W. and M. B. BRINKERHOFF (1974) "When proselytizing fails: an organizational analysis." Soc. Analysis 35: 189-200.

GORDON, D. (1974) "The Jesus people: an identity synthesis." Urban Life and Culture 3: 159-178.

HEIRICH, M. (1977) "Change of heart: a test of some widely held theories about religious conversion." Amer. J. of Sociology. (forthcoming)

KELLY, D. M. (1972) Why Conservative Churches are Growing. New York: Harper & Row.

KIESLER, C. A. (1971) The Psychology of Commitment: Experiments Linking Behavior and Belief. New York. Academic Press.

LISKA, A. E. (1977) "The dissipation of sociological social psychology." Amer. Sociologist 12: 2-8.

RICHARDSON, J. T. (1977) "Types of conversion and conversion careers in new religious movements." Paper read at the annual meeting of the American Association for the Advancement of Science, Denver, Colorado.

TAYLOR, B. (1976) "Conversion and cognition: an area for empirical study in the microsociology of religious knowledge." Social Compass 23: 5-22.

TRAVISANO, R. (1970) "Alternation and conversion as qualitatively different transformation," pp. 594-606 in G. P. Stone and M. Garverman (eds.) Social Psychology Through Symbolic Interaction. Waltham, MA: Ginn-Blaisdell.

ZYGMUNT, J. F. (1972) "Movements and motives: some unresolved issues in the psychology of social movements." Human Relations 25: 449-467.

Lofland's earlier work, widely assumed to have been done on the beginnings in this country of the Unification Church of Reverend Moon, resulted in development of the most widely cited conversion model in the literature of sociology. Here he updates and extends this previous work, based on a follow-up study of the same group studied earlier.

"Becoming a World-Saver" Revisited

JOHN LOFLAND
University of California, Davis

More than a decade ago, Stark and I observed a small number of then obscure millenarians go about what was to them the desperate and enormously difficult task of making converts. We witnessed techniques employed to foster conversion and observed the evolution of several people into converts. We strove to make some summarizing generalizations about those conversions in our report titled "Becoming a World-Saver" (Lofland and Stark, 1965), a report that has received a gratifying amount of attention over the years.

I want here to offer some new data on the conversion efforts of that same millenarian movement as it operates a decade later, to assess the new data's implications for the initial world-saver model, and to share some broader reflections on the model itself.

"DP" CONVERSION ORGANIZATION
REVISITED

The conversion efforts witnessed by Rodney Stark and myself in the early sixties were in many respects weak, hap-

JOHN LOFLAND's most recent books are *Doing Social Life, State Executions Viewed Historically and Sociologically* (with H. Bleackly), and *Social Strategies* (editor). He is currently Professor of Sociology at the University of California, Davis.

hazard, and bumbling. The gaining of a convert seemed often even to be an accident, a lucky conjunction of some rather random flailing (Lofland, 1966: Part II). Starting about 1972, however, all that was radically changed and transformed. The "DPs," as I continue to call them,[1] initiated what might eventually prove to be one of the most ingenious, sophisticated, and effective conversion organizations ever devised. I will describe its main phases and elements as it operated at and out of "State U City" and "Bay City," the same two West Coast places where the action centered in *Doomsday Cult* (Lofland, 1966).

DPs of the early sixties and seventies alike believed that their ideology was so "mind blowing" to unprepared citizens that they could not expect simply to announce its principle assertions and make converts at the same time. As documented throughout *Doomsday Cult,* effort was made to "hold back" the "conclusions" and only reveal them in a progressive and logical manner to prospective converts. They were dogged, that is, by a dilemma: they had to tell their beliefs in order to make converts, but the more they told the less likely was conversion.

They dealt with this dilemma by a carefully progressive set of revelations of their beliefs and aims, starting from complete muting or denial of the religious and millenarian aspects and ending with rather more disclosure. This process may be conceived as consisting of five, quasi-temporal phases: picking-up, hooking, encapsulating, loving, and committing,

PICKING-UP

Reports of people closely involved with the movement suggest that the multimillion dollar media blitzes and evangelical campaigns that made DPs famous and virtual household words in the seventies were not significant ways in which people began DP conversion involvement. Perhaps most commonly, it began with a casual contact in a public place, a "pickup." Indeed, DPs spent time almost daily giving hitchhikers rides and approaching young men and women in public places. Display card tables for front organizations[2] were regularly staffed in the public areas of many campuses as a way to pick up people.

The contact commonly involved an invitation to a dinner, a lecture, or both. Religious aspects would be muted or denied. As described in *Doomsday Cult* (Lofland, 1966: ch. 6), this strategy of covert presentations was employed in the early sixties with but small success. It became enormously more successful in the early seventies due to several larger-scale shifts in American society. First, the residue of the late sixties' rebellion of youth still provided a point of instant solidarity and trust among youth, especially in places like State U City, a major locale of public place pickups. Second, even though the number of drifting and alienated youth was declining from the late sixties, there were still plenty of them. They tended to be drawn to certain West Coast college towns and urban districts. DPs concentrated their pickups in such areas, with success.

While of major importance, pickups were not the sole strategy. Some minor and rudimentary infiltrations of religious gatherings continued (c.f. Lofland, 1966: 90-106), and one center specialized in sending "voluptuous and attractive" women to visit "professors at areas colleges and persuade them to come to meetings under the guise of Unified Science" (Bookin, 1973).

This shift in the strategy of first-contact and shifts in the larger trends of American society (see Lofland, 1977) resulted, further, in a decisive shift in the recruitment pool of the movement. Converts I studied in the early sixties were decidedly marginal and rather "crippled" people, drawn from the less than advantaged and more religiously inclined sectors of the social order. Hence, I quoted the Apostle Paul on the choosing of "mere nothings to overthow the existing order" (Lofland, 1966: 29). As it became fashionable in the late sixties and early seventies for privileged and secular youth of the higher social classes to be alienated from their society and its political and economic institutions, a portion of such youth encountered the DPs. Some converted. Some of them were offspring, indeed, of the American upper class, a fact that has caused the organization considerable trouble. What is signal here is that the major pattern of prior religious seeking I reported seemed to fade in significance. People with strong prior political perspectives and involvements (e.g.,

Eugene McCarthy workers) started converting. (Such changes must, of course, also be considered in conjunction with a growing political element within the DP itself.)

HOOKING

By whatever device, a prospect was brought into DP territory. Treatment varied at this point. In mid-1974 Chang himself was still experimenting in the New York City Center with Elmer's ancient notion of playing tape recorded lectures to people (Lofland, 1966: 125-129). Fortunately for recruitment to the movement, other centers went in different directions. The most successful hooked into their dinner and lecture guests with more intensive and elaborate versions of the "promotion tactics" I originally described in *Doomsday Cult* (Lofland, 1966: ch. 9). As practiced at the West Coast State U City Center—the most convert-productive center in the country—these went as follows.

1. The prospect arrived for dinner to find fifty or more smiling, talkative young people going about various chores. The place exuded friendliness and solicitude. He or she was assigned a "buddy" who was always by one's side. During the meal, as phrased in one report,

> various people stopped by my table, introduced themselves and chatted. They seemed to be circulating like sorority members during rush.

Members were instructed, indeed, to learn all they could about the prospect's background and opinions and to show personal interest. In one training document, members were told to ask: " 'What do you feel most excited about. . . .' *Write down* their hooks so that the whole center knows in follow up." The prospect's "buddy" and others continually complimented him: you have a happy or intelligent face; I knew I would meet someone great like you today; your shoes are nice; your sweater is beautiful; and so forth (c.f. Lofland, 1966: 175-177). The feeling, as one ex-member put it, was likely to be: "It certainly felt wonderful to be served, given such attention and made to feel important."

DPs, then, had learned to start conversion at the emotional rather than the cognitive level, an aspect they did not thoroughly appreciate in the early sixties (Lofland, 1966: 189).

2. It is on this foundation of positive affect that they slowly began to lay out their cognitive structure. That same first evening this took the form of a general, uncontroversial, and entertaining lecture on the "principles" that bound their Family group. Key concepts include sharing, loving one another, working for the good of humankind, and community activity (Taylor, 1975). Chang and his movement were never mentioned. At State U City (and several other places with the facilities), prospects were invited to a weekend workshop. This was conducted at The Farm in the State U City case I am following here, a several-hundred-acre country retreat some fifty miles north of Bay City. A slide show presented the attractions of The Farm. During the three years of most aggressive growth (1972-1974), probably several thousand people did a weekend at The Farm. Hundreds of others had kindred experiences elsewhere.

ENCAPSULATING

The weekend workshop (and longer subsequent periods) provided a solution to two former and major problems. First, by effectively encapsulating[3] prospects, the ideology could be progressively unfolded in a controlled setting, a setting where doubts and hesitations could be surfaced and rebutted. Second, affective bonds could be elaborated without interference from outsiders.

Focusing specifically on The Farm, the encapsulation of prospects moved along five fundamentally facilitating lines.

1. *Absorption of Attention.* All waking moments were pre-planned to absorb the participant's attention. The schedule was filled from 7:30 a.m. to 11:00 p.m. Even trips to the bathroom were escorted by one's assigned DP "buddy," the shadow who watched over his or her "spiritual child."

2. *Collective Focus.* A maximum of collective activities crowded the waking hours: group eating, exercises, garden work,

lectures, games, chantings, cheers, dancing, prayer, singing, and so forth. In such ways attention was focused outward and toward the group as an entity.

3. *Exclusive Input.* Prospects were not physically restrained, but leaving was strongly discouraged, and there were no newspapers, radios, TVs, or an easily accessible telephone. The Farm itself was miles from any settlement. Half of the fifty or so workshop participants were always DPs, and they dominated selection of topics for talk and what was said about them.

4. *Fatigue.* There were lectures a few hours each day, but the physical and social pace was otherwise quite intense. Gardening might be speeded up by staging contests, and games such as dodgeball were run at a frantic pitch. Saturday evening was likely to end with exhaustion, as in this report of interminable square-dancing.

> It went on for a very long time—I remember the beat of the music and the night air and thinking I would collapse and finding out I could go on and on. The feeling of doing that was really good—thinking I'd reached my limit and then pushing past it. [At the end, the leader] sang "Climb Every Mountain" in a beautiful, heartbreaking voice. Then we all had hot chocolate and went to bed.

A mild level of sexual excitement was maintained by frequent patting and hugging across the sexes. Food was spartan and sleep periods were controlled.

5. *Logical, Comprehensive Cognitions.* In this context, the DP ideology was systematically and carefully unfolded, from the basic and relatively bland principles (e.g., "give and take"; Lofland, 1966: 15-16) to the numerologically complex, from the Garden of Eden to the present day, following the pattern I reported in chapter 2 of *Doomsday Cult.* Indeed, if one accepted the premises from which it began, and were not bothered by several ad hoc devices, the system could seem exquisitely logical. The comprehensiveness combined with simplicity were apparently quite impressive to reasonable numbers of people who

viewed it in The Farm context. Indeed, the "inescapable" and "utterly logical" conclusion that the Messiah was at hand could hit hard: "It's so amazing, its so *scientific* and explains *everything.*"

The encapsulating and engrossing quality of these weekends was summed up well by one almost-convert:

> The whole weekend had the quality of a cheer—like one long rousing camp song. What guests were expected (and subtly persuaded) to do was participate . . . completely. That was stressed over and over: "give your whole self and you'll get a lot back," "the only way for this to be the most wonderful experience of your life is if you really put everything you have into it," etc.

LOVING

But the core element of this process was deeper and more profound than any of the foregoing. Everything mentioned so far only in part moved a person toward a position in which they were open to what was the crux: the feeling of being loved and the desire to "melt together" (a movement concept) into the loving, enveloping embrace of the collective. (Indeed, we learn again from looking at the DPs that love can be the most coercive and cruel power of all.)

The psychodynamic of it is so familiar as to be hackneyed: "people need to belong, to feel loved," as it is often put. People who want to "belong" and do not, or who harbor guilt over their reservations about giving themselves over to collectivities, are perhaps the most vulnerable to loving overtures toward belonging. The pattern has been stated with freshness and insight by a young, recently-Christian woman who did a Farm weekend, not then knowing she was involved with the DPs:

> When I did hold back in some small way, and received a look of sorrowful, benevolent concern, I felt guilt and the desire to please as though it were God Himself whom I had offended. What may really have been wisdom on my part (trying to preserve my own boundaries in a dangerous and potentially overwhelming situation) was treated as symptomatic of alienation and fear; and a withholding of God's light. Those things are sometimes true of me, and I am unsure enough of my own openness in groups that

I tended to believe they were right. Once, when [the workshop leader] spoke to us after a lecture, I began to cry. She'd said something about giving, and it had touched on a deep longing in me to do that, and the pain of that wall around my heart when I feel closed off in a group of people. I wanted to break through that badly enough that right then it almost didn't matter what they believed—if only I could really share myself with them. I think that moment may be exactly the point at which many people decide to join [the DPs].

The conscious strategy of these encapsulating weekend camps was to drench prospects in approval and love—to "love bomb" them, as DPs termed it. The cognitive hesitations and emotional reservations of prospects could then be drowned in calls to loving solidarity:

Whenever I would raise a theological question, the leaders of my group would look very impressed and pleased, seem to agree with me, and then give me a large dose of love—and perhaps say something about unity and God's love being most important. I would have an odd, disjointed sort of feeling—not knowing if I'd really been heard or not, yet aware of the attentive look and the smiling approval. My intellectual objection had been undercut by means of emotional seduction.

Or sometimes the group would burst into song: "We love you, Julie; oh, yes we do; we don't love anyone as much as you." I read it this way: we *could* love you if you weren't so naughty. And, of course, they *would* love her.

This incredibly intense encapsulating and loving did not simply "happen." DPs trained specifically for it and held morale and strategy sessions among themselves during the workshops:

On Sunday morning, when I woke really early, I walked by the building where some of the Family members had slept. They were up and apparently having a meeting. I heard a cheer: "Gonna meet all their needs." And that did seem to be what they tried to do. Whatever I wanted—except privacy or any deviation from the schedule—would be gotten for me immediately and with great concern. I was continually smiled at, hugged, patted. And I was made to feel very special and very much wanted.

As characterized by investigative reporter Ross, people were "picked up from an emotional floor and taken care of." "The appeal is love—blissed out harmony and unity" (Ross, 1975). Indeed, Ross and his coworkers discovered some converts who had been in the movement four to six months who truly seemed to have attended to little or nothing regarding Chang and his larger movement. They were simply part of a loving commune. Some, on being pressed explicitly with Chang's beliefs and aims, declared they did not care: their loyalty was to the family commune. Such, as Stark and I discussed with regard to "affective bonds," is an important meaning of love (Lofland and Stark, 1965: 871-872).

COMMITTING

It is one thing to get "blissed out" on a group over a weekend, but is another thing to give one's life over to it. And the DPs did not seem immediately to ask that one give over one's life. Instead, the blissed-out prospect was invited to stay on at The Farm for a week-long workshop. And if that worked out, one stayed for an even longer period. The prospect was drawn gradually—but in an encapsulated setting—into full working, street peddling, and believing participation.

Doubts expressed as time went on were defined as "acts of Satan" (Lofland, 1966: 193-198), and the dire consequence of then leaving the movement would be pointed out (Lofland, 1966: 185-188). A large portion of new converts seemed not to have had extramovement ties to worry about, but those who did—such as having concerned parents—seemed mostly to be encouraged to minimize the import of their DP involvement to such outsiders and thereby to minimize the threat it might pose to them.

A part of the process of commitment seemed to involve a felt cognitive dislocation arising from the intense encapsulating and loving. One prospect, an almost-convert who "broke off" from his "buddy" after a weekend, reported:

"As soon as I left Suzie," he said, "I had a chance to think, to analyze what had happened and how everything was controlled. I felt free and alive again—it was like a spell was broken."

Another, on being sent out to sell flowers after three weeks at The Farm, had this experience:

> Being out in the world again was a shock; a cultural shock in which I was unable to deal with reality. My isolation by the Church had been so successful that everyday sights such as hamburger stands and TVs, even the people, looked foreign, of another world. I had been reduced to a dependent being! The Church had seen to it that my three weeks with them made me so vulnerable and so unable to cope with the real world, that I was compelled to stay with them.

This "spell," "trance," or "shock" experience is not as foreign, strange, or unique as it might, at first viewing, appear. People exiting any highly charged involvement—be it a more ordinary love affair, raft trip, two-week military camp, jail term, or whatever—are likely to experience what scientists of these matters have called "the reentry problem" (Irwin, 1970: ch. 5). Reentry to any world after absence is in many circumstances painful, and a desire to escape from that pain increases the attractiveness of returning to the just-prior world. Especially because the DP situation involved a supercharged love and support experience, we ought to expect people to have reentry unreality, to experience enormous discontinuity and a desire to flee back. DPs created their own attractive kind of "high"—of transcending experience—to which people could perhaps be drawn back in much the same way Lindesmith has argued people employ certain drugs to avoid withdrawal (reentry pains?) as well as exploiting them for their own inherently positive effects (Lindesmith, 1968; Lofland with Lofland, 1969: 104-116).

THE WORLD-SAVER MODEL
REVISITED

A first and prime question is, of course: what are the implications of the above for the world-saver model that Stark and I evolved from an earlier era of DP conversion organization? As summarized in the report's abstract, the model propounds that:

> For conversion a person must experience, within a religious problem-solving perspective, enduring, acutely-felt tensions that lead him to define himself as a religious seeker; he must encounter the cult at a turning point in his life; within the cult an affective bond must be formed (or pre-exist) and any extra-cult attachments, neutralized; and there he must be exposed to intensive interaction if he is to become a "deployable agent." [Lofland and Stark, 1965: 862]

My impression is that the situational elements of the model, at least, are so general and abstract that they can, with no difficulty, also accurately (but grossly) characterize the newer DP efforts. Indeed, they are general and abstract to the point of not being especially telling, perhaps reflecting the rather pallid data with which Stark and I had to work. The play of movement and external "affective bonds" and "intensive interaction" continues, certainly, but the new DP efforts now permit much more refined and sophisticated analysis, a level of refinement and sophistication at which I have only been able to hint in my descriptions of "encapsulating" and "loving." I believe, in fact, that close study of the two major DP conversion camps could result in a quantum step in our understanding of conversion, for the DPs have elaborated some incredible nuances.

Relative to the more "background" elements, the concept of the "turning point" is troublesome because everyone can be seen as in one or more important ways at a turning point at every moment of their lives. Like concepts of tension, it is true and interesting but not very cutting. As mentioned, there seems to have been a definite broadening of the range of people who get into the DP. The pattern of prior and universal religious seeking, at least in its narrow form, became far less than universal. People not previously religious at all have joined in noticeable numbers. Only further study can sort out the contexts and meanings underlying the diverse new patterns. Further study ought to address, however, the possibility that an entire generation of youth became, broadly speaking, religious seekers in the early seventies and frenzied themselves, indeed, with a fashion of "seeker chic," a sibling of Wolfe's (Wolfe, 1976) aptly identified "funky chic." Last, there seems no reason to modify our polymorphic characterization of "tension," which remains, however, a feature that is virtually universal in the human population.

Be all of that as it may, let me now step back and view the world-saver model as an instance of *qualitative process theorizing.* I have been impressed that, although there have been efforts to give the model a quantitative testing, to employ it in organizing materials on conversion to other groups, and to state the correlates of conversion, almost no one has tried their own hand at qualitative process models of conversion. The world-saver model was intended as much as an analytic description of a sequence of experiences as it was as a "causal theory," and it was very much informed by Turner's (1953: 609-611) too-neglected formulation of the distinction between "closed systems" and "intrusive factors." That kind of logic clearly has not caught on, despite the oddity that much lip-service is given to it, and the world-saver model provides an example of it, as do the very widely known and generically identical models of Becker (1953) on marihuana use, Cressey (1972) on trust violation, and Smelser (1963) on collective behavior. Indeed, and I think now in error, my own effort to generalize the world-saver model to all deviant identities lapsed into the mere causal-factorial approach in providing eleven social organizational variations that affect the likelihood of assuming a deviant identity and reversing it (Lofland with Lofland, 1969: Parts II and III). Such an approach is fine and necessary, but it is a retreat from the study of process, a retreat signaled in my all too abstract, brief, and shakily founded depiction of "escalating interaction" (Lofland with Lofland, 1969: 146-154).

I would have hoped that by now we might have at least half a dozen qualitative process models of conversion, each valid for the range and kind of event it addressed, and each offering insights, even if not the most sophisticated account that might be given. We then could be well on our way to talking about types of conversion and types of qualitative conversion processes. Instead, I fear, some investigators get hung up in trying to determine if the world-saver model is "right" as regards the group they have studied. In my view, such investigators would advance us better by looking at the conversion process directly and reporting what they saw. Stark and I did not feel it necessary to wear anyone's specific model when we went to look at conversion. I would urge now that people ought not so compulsively wear the tinted spectacles wrought by Lofland and Stark when they go to look at conversion. I would urge, that is, a knowledge of the logic of a qualitative process point of view, but an eschewing of harassing oneself to look at the world through a specific application of that logic (see further, Lofland, 1976: Part 1).

Stepping back yet further, I have since come to appreciate that the world-saver model embodies a thoroughly "passive" actor—a conception of humans as a "neutral medium through which social forces operate," as Blumer (1969) has so often put it. The world-saver model is actually quite antiinteractionist, or at least anti the interactionism frequently identified with people such as Blumer.

It is with such a realization that I have lately encouraged students of conversion to turn the process on its head and to scrutinize how people go about converting themselves. Assume, that is, that the person is active rather than merely passive (Lofland, 1976: ch. 5). Straus' (1976) "Changing Oneself: Seekers and the Creative Transformation of Life Experience" is an important initial effort to lay down new pathways of analysis within such an activist-interactionist perspective. I hope there will soon be many efforts of its kind.

Looking back from the perspective of a decade, however, I think students of conversion have ample reason for celebration and optimism. Stark and I had very few models and theoretical and substantive material to guide us. Limitations aside, there is now a rather solid and rich body of reasonably specific ideas and data-bits that can guide investigators. We do now know more about conversion than we did a decade ago, and I have every confidence that we will know enormously more a decade hence.

NOTES

1. Because of DP fame, my pseudonyms are now somewhat labored, but I must continue to protect the anonymity of the movement for the reasons indicated in Lofland (1977: note 1).

The main phases of the development of the DP movement from 1959 through 1976 are chronicled in my "Preface" to the Irvington edition of *Doomsday Cult* (Lofland, 1977). Transformations in membership size and composition, modes of operation, funding, and other aspects are equally as startling as the changes in conversion organization I report here.

My account is drawn from the diverse sources described in Lofland (1977: note 2), save here again to acknowledge the indispensable help of Andrew Ross, Michael Greany, David Taylor, and Hedy Bookin.

2. DPs evolved dozens of front organizations from behind which they carried on an amazing variety of movement-promoting activities (see Lofland, 1977: phase two, section IV, "Missionizing").

3. I use the concept of "encapsulation" here in a related but not identical manner to that introduced in analysis of deviant act (Lofland with Lofland, 1969: 39-60).

REFERENCES

BECKER, H. S. (1953) "Becoming a marihuana user." Amer. J. of Sociology 59: 235-242.

BLUMER, H. (1969) Symbolic Interactionism. Englewood Cliffs, NJ: Prentice-Hall.

BOOKIN, H. (1972-1976) Private notes and personal communications.

CRESSEY, D. R. (1972) Other People's Money. Belmont, CA: Wadsworth.

IRWIN, J. (1970) The Felon. Englewood Cliffs, NJ: Prentice-Hall.

LOFLAND, J. (1977) "The boom and bust of a millenarian movement: doomsday cult revisited." Preface to the Irvington edition of J. Lofland, Doomsday Cult. New York: Irvington.

——— (1976) Doing Social Life: The Qualitative Study of Human Interaction in Natural Settings. New York: John Wiley.

——— (1966) Doomsday Cult: A Study of Conversion, Proselytization, and Maintenance of Faith. Englewood Cliffs, NJ: Prentice-Hall.

——— with the assistance of L. H. LOFLAND (1969) Deviance and Identity. Englewood Cliffs, NJ: Prentice-Hall.

LOFLAND, J. and R. STARK (1965) "Becoming a world-saver: a theory of conversion to a deviant perspective." Amer. Soc. Rev. 30: 862-874.

ROSS, A. (1975-1976) Private notes and personal communications.

SMELSER, N. J. (1963) Theory of Collective Behavior. New York: Free Press.

STRAUS, R. (1976) "Changing oneself: seekers and the creative transformation of life experience," pp. 252-272 in J. Lofland, Doing Social Life. New York: John Wiley.

TAYLOR, D. (1975-1976) Private notes and personal communications.

TURNER, R. H. (1953) "The quest for universals in sociological research." Amer. J. of Sociology 18: 604-611.

WOLFE, T. (1976) Mauve Gloves & Madmen, Clutter & Vine. New York: Farrar, Straus & Giroux.

This paper is an extension of previous process models of conversion, based on research on the Jesus movement. The detailed examination of "predispositions" for conversion and the discussion of the importance of affective ties in the conversion process are of particular interest.

Conversion Process Models and the Jesus Movement

JAMES T. RICHARDSON
University of Nevada, Reno

MARY STEWART
University of Missouri

The last decade or so in American life can be characterized as an "age of conversion." Literally hundreds of thousands of people, many but not all of them relatively young, have been involved in experiences of shifting alliances among various groups and ideologies. This pattern of changing from one group to another by large numbers of people does not fit the usual approach to understanding conversion. Traditionally, conversion has been viewed as something that happens once in a lifetime, in either an abrupt or a gradual fashion, with the person usually staying converted to the same perspective for a noticeable length of time. Such a view of conversion has been made problematic by the events of the past few years. What is needed is an approach to conversion that takes into account the "multievent con-

---

Authors' Note: *A version of part of this paper was presented earlier at the Annual Meeting of the Pacific Sociological Association in Scottsdale, Arizona. That paper was revised during a year spent at the London School of Economics by the first author, who was on a sabbatical. Appreciation is expressed for the sabbatical and for the kindness shown by L.S.E.*

JAMES T. RICHARDSON is Professor of Sociology at the University of Nevada, Reno. His major present research interests include the sociology of religion and social movements. He has studied new religious groups in America and overseas for several years, focusing on the Jesus movement and the neo-Pentecostal movement.

MARY STEWART is Assistant Professor of Sociology at the University of Missouri, Kansas City. Her current research interests include child abuse, sociology of women, and battered women.

[24]

versions" of recent times, and also the fact that the large number of conversions occurred for many different reasons. Also, it has become apparent that the process models of conversion and commitment in the sociological literature are not adequate explanations of the complex conversion events of these times. Put differently, even if we temporarily suspend our knowledge that many recent conversions are multiple-event phenomena, and that a single conversion event is but one step in a possibly rather lengthy sequence of conversion events, we are still left with problems explaining the single conversion event on which we might be focusing.

This situation results from the fact that major theoretical tools developed by social scientists working in this field were usually developed by focusing on just one or two relatively atypical groups. For instance, the most widely cited such model, that of Lofland and Stark (1965), was developed using only a few case studies of people who were typically older "social misfits" from different social locations than the preponderance of participants in the "age of protest" of the middle and late 1960s. Another often-cited model, that of Gerlach and Hine (1970), was derived from a study of neo-Pentecostalism, with its usually older converts, and the "black power" movement, with its black participants.

This conclusion about the inadequacy of available conversion or commitment models has been arrived at inductively. We have done research on one particular new religious movement—the Jesus movement (JM)—and we have attended to the growing literature about other new religious movements (some of which are represented in this volume). Our early research was guided by concerns about the conversion process because of interest in discerning which people were affiliating with the new movements and the process whereby such people came to affiliate with groups that made up the movements. That interest manifested itself in two ways early in our research. One was to apply "brain-washing" or "thought reform" models to the JM (Richardson et al., 1972), an exercise that was of interest because of the growing accusations that "brain-washing" was indeed being used in recruitment by some of the groups (see Shupe et al., in this volume). Another was to apply popular conversion models from the sociological literature to the JM in an effort to test the models and to learn more about what was happening in the movement vis-à-vis conversion processes. The most potentially valuable model, that of Lofland and Stark (1965), has seldom been tested as such.[1] Lofland and Stark do not claim that their model is general; however, it has been treated by others as a widely applicable one. For this reason, we decided to use the Lofland and Stark model as a major element in our study of conversion to new religious movements.

What follows here is a much-shortened version of our work in this area (for the "full treatment," see Richardson et al., 1977), with the primary focus being to extend conversion process models into a more general model to explain "single-event" conversions, not only as they occur in the JM, but in other contemporary movements as well. Obviously, such an effort will contribute as well as to explaining "multievent conversion" and "conversion careers" (see Richardson, 1977).

In what follows, we will be using information mainly from our own Jesus movement research, which has been continuing since 1971, focusing on one large, nationwide JM group. More recent attention has been given by the first author to another JM group—the widely discussed Children of God (see Davis and Richardson, 1976). Also, the first author has been involved with research overseas on the neo-Pentecostal movement (see Richardson and Reidy, 1976, forthcoming; and Reidy and Richardson, 1975, 1977). These research projects have involved participant observation, content analysis of documents, interviews, and—especially with the first group mentioned—the use of survey and personality assessment instruments (see Harder et al., 1972, 1976; Harder, 1974; Simmonds et al., 1974, 1976 for examples of reports based directly on the survey and personality assessment instruments). In all of this research a part of the effort was directed at discovering the types of people who affiliated and the conversion-commitment processes used in the various groups.

SUMMARY OF LOFLAND AND STARK MODEL

Before proceeding, we need to summarize the best of past work on which we will build. Lofland and Stark (1965), after extensive study of a small eclectic religious group called the "Divine Precepts," outlined seven factors, the *accumulation of which* is both a necessary and a sufficient cause for conversion. They conceived of conversion as a *funneling and shifting process,* the elements of which are *not* considered to be ordered in terms of temporal occurrence. Rather, the ordering principle is one of "activation."[2]

The following factors were seen as necessary background or *predisposing characteristics:*

(1) perception of considerable long-term tension, strain, deprivation, or frustration (felt needs),

(2) possession of a "religious" rhetoric and problem-solving perspective (contrasted to "political" or "psychiatric" perspectives, which are "secular definitions"),

(3) self-definition as "religious seeker" (involves rejection of traditional religion, and the more "secular" definitions as solutions to felt problems).

The *situational factors* arising from interaction between potential converts and cult members were seen by Lofland and Stark to be essential factors in the conversion process:

(4) "turning point" reached (old lines of action no longer operable, and contact with a cult member begins),

(5) development (or preexistence) of affective bonds between "preconvert" and cult members (serious consideration of cult ideology begins),

(6) relatively weak or neutralized extracult affective ties (or existent ties were with other "seekers" who encourage continued contact)—culminates in "verbal conversion,"

(7) intensive (usually communal) interaction with cult members culminates in "total conversion," and person becomes "deployable agent."

CRITIQUE AND EXTENSION OF
THE CONCEPT OF "PREDISPOSITIONS"

Although Lofland and Stark explicitly and insightfully focus on predispositions, possibly because of their population of study they do not develop the idea as much as seems needed in studying contemporary movements. We think that (1) they delineated too few basic perspectives, (2) the concept of a basic perspective was not developed as fully as it might have been, (3) the perspectives used were viewed as relatively static, and (4) the implications for and complexity of the "religious" perspective in terms of its contribution to "felt tensions" was not made explicit.

ADDITIONAL PERSPECTIVES

At least one major "new" perspective needs to be added to Lofland and Stark's three, and another, briefly discussed in their work, should be more carefully explicated if the model is to be made more applicable to contemporary conversion phenomena. These "new" perspectives are in addition to (but at the same level of abstraction as) their three—the *psychiatric,* the *political,* and the *religious*—only one of which, the religious, was used in a major explanatory way in their research. The brief definitions given these three perspectives by Lofland and Stark (1965: 867) were:

> In the first (psychiatric), the origin of problems is typically traced to the psyche, and manipulation of the self is advocated as a solution. Political solutions, mainly radical, locate the sources of problems in the social structure and advocate reorganization of the system as a solution. The religious perspective tends to see both sources and solutions as emanating from an unseen, and in principle, unseeable realm.

We suggest, based on our research into the past history of JM converts, the addition of a physiological perspective, which is defined as including the use of elements or activities to affect the body and mind in ways that furnish some meaning for the person. One might be tempted to refer to this perspective as hedonistic or "withdrawal," but to do so would belie the serious and active approach to life taken by many participants we encountered in our research. Also, such terms as "withdrawal" have a generally negative connotation, and we prefer a non-normative stance on such issues. While the physiological perspective may include as important elements the use of sex and drugs, there are other activities that also can and should be classified as a part of this view of life. For instance, the use of alcohol and such things as health food "trips," dieting, vitamins, exercise, and other "body therapies" also should be included. The over-riding tie among such activities is the doing of things that somehow include and affect the body in an attempt to achieve meaning, whether that meaning is derived from orgasms, jogging, natural foods, or some innovative combination of such activities.

Another important perspective might be termed the "muddle through" or conventional perspective. Lofland and Stark (1965: 867) write: "Because people have a number of conventional and readily available definitions for, and means of coping with their problems, there were, in the end, very few converts to D.P." Later, they mention some "normal" things that potential converts can do to alleviate their situations short of conversion: "persist in stressful situations with little or no relief," or "take specifically problem-directed action to change troublesome portions of their lives, without adopting a different world view to interpret them," or take advantage of "a number of maneuvers to 'put the problem out of mind'" (Lofland and Stark, 1965: 868). This latter situation they describe as "compensations for or distractions from problems of living," and they specifically mention such things as mass media addiction, child-rearing, immersion in work, and, more spectacularly, alcoholism, suicide, and promiscuity. We would add a few more examples of the use of a conventional perspective to solve problems—such things as getting a divorce, getting married, moving, changing jobs, taking a holiday, dropping out of school, and affiliating with a conventional religious (or other type of) group (or changing such affiliation). The basic thrust of this idea is that there are more or less acceptable ways that most people interpret and deal with problems. Most people probably try to muddle through before dealing with their problem in more dramatic ways. Muddling through may well be something of a quiescent state to which people regularly return when more dramatic solutions are not viewed as available.

DIFFERENT LEVELS OF ANALYSIS

Thus, we suggest five major perspectives for interpreting and dealing with felt problems—*psychiatric, political, religious, physiological, and conventional*—all conceptualized at the same level of abstraction. However, it seems plain that there are various ways of viewing these several perspectives, fitting them into what, for want of a better term, we will designate *general orientations.* Lofland and Stark talk about their three perspectives in such a manner, referring to both the political and the psychiatric as being "secular," but they do not develop this idea.

One seemingly fruitful way to view the several perspectives is to focus on the most basic unit used in defining problems and solutions to problems. This leads us to the use of the admittedly simplistic but still valuable dichotomy of *individualism-collectivism.* This differentiation is given considerable import by some (see Martin, 1965, and Richardson, 1974). All but one of the five perspectives would usually be classified as an *individualistic* approach to defining and solving felt problems. Only the political perspective, particularly as defined by Lofland and Stark to mean more radical political views, seems even potentially classifiable as a *collectivistic world view.*[3]

This notion of general orientations suggests that individuals with "felt difficulties" typically would be expected to follow certain "conversion careers." For instance, a person might be expected to shift from one alternative to another *within a given basic perspective* before trying another general orientation. Travisano's (1970) distinction (further discussed in Richardson, 1977) between "alternation" and "conversion" seems apropos here. Conversion would apply to the case of "movement" *between* general orientations, and perhaps to some movements within a general orientation, if the basic perspectives are relatively "far apart" (i.e., if some important content elements of the basic perspectives were antithetical to each other). Alternations (movement *within* a general orientation) would seem less problematic than conversions, a situation with import in terms of the processes involved. An alternation would typically seem easier to accomplish than a conversion, and, thus, more alternations might be expected.[4] The work of Gordon (1974) and our work support this idea, as few "true conversions" (change of general orientation) were found.

STATIC VERSUS DYNAMIC APPROACHES

Lofland and Stark seem rather static in their approach to basic perspectives (and general orientations), a situation probably deriving from the type of people being studied—people with an inculcated "religious" perspective who were affiliating with a somewhat deviant religious group. The only shift involved is *within* an orientation and perspective that we would categorize as "individualistic." Other "solutions" to felt problems cited by Lofland and Stark also involve shifts within an individualistic orientation (e.g., suicide, moving house, and so on). They recognize that they are not talking about other types of shifts, for they say:

> We think the model suggests some rudiments of a general account of conversion to deviant perspectives. But the degree to which this scheme applies to shifts between widely held perspectives must, for now, remain problematic. [Lofland and Stark, 1965: 826]

The lack of fundamental shifting across general orientation boundaries in the DP converts was evidenced in comments about the social origins of most converts and the type of perspective held by the converts studied. Most converts were "primarily white, Protestant, and young (typically below 35); some had college training, and most were Americans of lower middle-class and small-town origins" (Lofland and Stark, 1965: 863). Lofland and Stark (1965: 869) claimed that the "concrete preconvert beliefs varied a good deal," a point we would caution readers against overinterpreting, as most if not all "preconverts" apparently shared a religious view usually thought of as individualistic. Preconverts shared

> postulates about the nature of ultimate reality. . . . First, they believed that spirits of some variety come from an active supernatural realm to intervene in the "material world." . . . Second, their conception of the universe was technological . . . each person must have been "put on earth" for some reason. [Lofland and Stark, 1965: 869]

Thus, it appears that there had not been a major shift in orientation for "DP" converts that would, in our terms, mean a change from an individualistic to a collectivistic orientation (or vice-versa).

To illustrate the basic dynamism of many contemporary "conversions," a few comments about "multievent" conversions seem in order (see Richardson, 1977, for more on this phenomenon). Our work (and Gordon, 1974) demonstrates the prevalence of multiple-event conversions. To help account for the great amount of *ideological mobility* that has been typical of some groups and individuals in contemporary society, we suggest a concept of *serial alternatives*.[5] This concept (which has some similarities to the notion of "serial monogamy" as a way of characterizing modern marriage) seems to incorporate the dynamic element in modern-day conversion phenomena and will, we think, incorporate shifts within a perspective, from one perspective to another, and from one general orientation to another. We live in a time-space social environment that is a virtual "supermarket of ideas" which might be characterized as a large and differentiated *opportunity structure* of possible ways to interpret and resolve felt problems. And the social situation of the 1960s virtually guaranteed that many new "solutions" would be defined into existence, and that, paradoxically, few of them would be defined as lasting solutions for members of certain social groups. Thus, many people moved from one alternative to another, in a serial fashion.

Given the common social origins and personal experiences of most participants in the JM, it seems possible to construct typical *conversion career* patterns for participants. Adams and Fox (1972), in one research report that briefly addresses this question, found such patterns, although they do not give enough detail to allow a thorough test of our idea. They were surprised with their findings, as the following quote illustrates:

> Before beginning this study, the writers had theorized that Jesus people who are ex-dopers had participated in a succession of social movements: they began in the peace movement, had dropped out into the drug scene, and finally joined the religious revival. The data, however, refute this assumption about the sequence of membership in the various movements for the use of drugs almost always preceded participation in the peace movement.

Thus, a typical though unexpected "conversion career" for a majority of their respondents was discernible, and they also found other patterns in other "classes" of respondents. Gordon (1974) found discernible typical "conversion careers" in his study of a small Chicago JM group, and we, too, noted certain common patterns in our research.

Such conversion patterns are not random for the Jesus movement, and probably for no other group or movement as well. We think it possible to develop a rather sophisticated, even somewhat "math-model" approach to this problem of conversion—an approach that could perhaps associate probabilities with certain conversion patterns or "trajectories," and with certain types of conversion *within* a pattern, since many patterns would probably involve several conversions (see the somewhat similar approach by Parrucci, 1968, and also the learning theory approach by Weiss, 1963, to explaining conversion patterns).

The basic elements of such a dynamic model would probably fall into three broad categories: (1) prior socialization, (2) contemporaneous experiences and circumstances, and (3) the opportunity structure available for problem definition and resolution.[6] Prior socialization is related to predispositions, in that all individuals are inculcated with basic perspectives and orientations which they apply in their life, but may sometimes modify. A change or disavowal of such a perspective usually results from a negative interpretation being given to contemporaneous experiences and circumstances, and the change must occur within available alternatives.

IMPLICATIONS OF A
CERTAIN RELIGIOUS PERSPECTIVE

We will now examine, in an admittedly speculative way, one particular "way" of raising a child that was, we think, of considerable import in Lofland and Stark's research, and in our own. The "way" of import to both studies is that of fundamentalist or conservative Christianity. It seems probable that many if not most of Lofland and Stark's 15 subjects had such a religious background. Their small-town, lower middle-class, Protestant origins seem congruent with such a notion, as does the characterization of their basic perspective, which we have already discussed. An added point of support from their beliefs is that they believed in Satan an active spirit (Lofland and Stark, 1965: 869). Also, most descriptions of the Jesus movement have characterized the movement as fundamentalist (see Enroth et al., 1972, for example). Such descriptions raise an interesting question: could it be that, contrary to some popular discussions of the movement, most of the members are "returning fundamentalists"?

Our research and that of Gordon (1974) suggest that such is quite possible, and this idea, coupled with knowledge that most of Lofland and Stark's converts were probably also originally conservative or fundamentalist Protestants, suggest yet another line of inquiry. Is it possible that such a background makes people more predisposed toward deviant affiliations? Does such a perspective usually result in more personal problems in such an age as this, where a fundamentalist world view is in the minority?[7] And does the fundamentalist world view contain elements that made such a world view especially subject to refutation during the turmoil of the 1960s in America? If the answer to the last question is "yes," then we are faced with the paradoxical situation of being led to suggest that fundamentalism—that "rock from whence most of us were hewn"—may actually have *contributed to* the severe problems which developed in the 1960s in America (and it also seems to be contributing to the "solution" of the severe problems, which adds to the paradox).

Needless to say, this view of the meaning of religious background for the conversion process differs from the emphasis in Lofland and Stark that such experiences contribute "only" a religious perspective. Such a difference of meaning needs to be examined in more detail, but space limitations preclude such treatment here (see Richardson et al., 1977, for more discussion of this idea).

However, we would speculate that being raised as a fundamentalist possibly makes people more prone to encounter frustration in their lives in modern society. This idea receives support from the work of Fromm (1950), in which he makes his classic distinction between authoritarian and humanitarian religions. Fromm, whose definition of authoritarian religion seems to fit fundamentalism, offers an element, Marxian in derivation, of "self-alienation" to our study. He says (1950: 53): "The real fall of man is his alienation from himself, his submission to power, his turning against himself even though under the guise of worship of God." His description is of a person debilitated by a set of beliefs that degrade man and lead to dependency. Such a person would be prone to encounter problems living in a world such as ours, caught up in such rapid change and disorder. The thorough work of Pattison (1970) on fundamentalism is also supportive of this view.[8]

Such a view receives some support from Lofland and Stark's (1965: 867) claim that, although felt problems objectively did not appear to be overly severe, "pre-converts felt their problems were quite acute, and they experienced high levels of tension concerning them over long periods." The authors never made a connection between prior religious socialization and present tension-filled state of their converts. Instead, they (1965: 867) asserted: "Most people probably have some type of frustrated aspiration, but the pre-converts *experienced* the tension rather more acutely and over longer periods than most people do."

Perhaps fundamentalism represents an important case of what Toch (1965: 128-129) refers to as "oversocialization." He notes that all converts are previously disillusioned people, and defines a dillusioning experience as "the perception of discrepancy between conventional beliefs and psychological and physical realities." His description of the types of beliefs and situations resulting in disillusionment for certain types of people seems apropos of fundamentalism. He summarizes his discussion of the types of beliefs, situations, and people by saying: "a person will tend to become disillusioned if he becomes actively involved in life situations for which he has been ill-prepared by socialization" (Toch, 1965: 128). He then closes his provocative discussion of "oversocialization" with a paragraph that seems to have been written with fundamentalism and the JM in mind:

> Although there are many deficits in the socialization process, its most general defect is overambitiousness. Persons who have been oversocialized, in the sense that too many absolutes have been inculcated in them, are most likely to experience subsequent clashes with reality. The extreme instance of this rule is the true believer, for whom life becomes a constant struggle to impose shakey dogmas on slippery facts. In general, a person who demands that conventional society conform to his mold soon finds that he must either revise his expectations or transform the social order. He may try both. [Toch, 1965: 128-129]

SITUATIONAL FACTORS IN CONVERSION

We have focused mainly on the Lofland and Stark model of conversion in the discussion of predisposing characteristics. We will now briefly examine one aspect of *situational factors* in conversion, an analytical area that includes the latter several elements of the Lofland and Stark (1965) model, virtually all of the model developed by Gerlach and Hine (1970), the valuable broader work of White (1968), and McHugh's (1970) related work on resocialization, among others.

One especially important situational factor is that of the formation of *affective ties* between potential converts and group members. This variable has been deemed of great import by most writers in the conversion literature, but its operation has not been adequately specified for contemporary conversion phenomena (see Balch and Taylor, in this issue, for one attempt). Gerlach and Hine note that conversion usually occurs to specific "cells" of movement, not to movements as a whole, and Lofland and Stark's study illustrates this key point, as does our own work. Affective ties must usually be developed between a potential convert and members of a specific group to which that potential convert may be predisposed, for whatever the reason. Affective ties to group members do not necessarily preclude affective ties between potential converts and people outside the group, but probably a situation of weak ties with nongroup members, such as those with whom one would usually be expected to have positive affective ties (family members, spouses, classmates, and the like), would contribute to the propensity of a person to convert, as is assumed by Lofland and Stark, among others.

An important interaction of affective ties with a group and nongroup members might occur when a nongroup member with whom the potential convert had positive affective ties was positive (or at least neutral) toward the group which an individual was considering joining. In such an instance a positive affective tie with someone *outside* the group might actually *contribute* to conversion. A similar effect *might* be found if a *negative* affect with significant nongroup others was associated with a *negative* evaluation of the group by the nongroup other(s). This line of thought, which seems to extend theorizing about the operation of the variable of affective ties with nongroup members, gained some suggestive support in our research. We encountered a number of members whose parents or significant others were positive toward the group and encouraged the convert to join *and* to stay affiliated. Perhaps this effect occurs only with groups that are closely related to the dominant culture, as are the JM and the neo-Pentecostal movement. Much more research is needed on this intriguing finding, however, before conclusions can be drawn.

RELATING PREDISPOSITIONS
AND AFFECTIVE TIES

Table 1 presents in summary form some possible relationships between predisposing elements or factors and affective ties with group members.[9] Admittedly, the variables in the table are simplified abstractions, but nonetheless we hope the tabular scheme conveys the importance of both predisposing and situational (or, to use Zygmunt's, 1972, terms, motivational and interactional) variables, and indicates that conversion can occur in qualitatively different situations. Note that while "congruence" is used mainly as a cognitive kind of variable, we would suggest that the term would also include behavioral elements as well (see Kiesler, 1971).

Plainly, individuals (or groups) classifiable in cell one of the table would be most prone to convert, while those in cell nine would be less prone to convert. Ranking the rest of the cells on a continuum of "proneness to convert" is more problematic, however. Lofland and Stark's work, with its emphasis on predisposing factors, seems to imply that those in cell two might be relatively prone to convert, whereas Gerlach and Hine's work seems to suggest that those in cells one, four, and seven would be about equally prone to convert, although it should be said that Gerlach and Hine do not explicitly take a variable such as "congruence" into account in their scheme, which seems to imply that "initial contact" and "refocusing of needs" (two elements of their scheme) operate the same on most people. Both models (and White, 1968) suggest that those falling into cells three, six, and nine will not convert.

Two comments should be made about the operation of the major variables in the table. First, individuals may "move" over time to different cells in the table. People may change their affective ties with group members (indeed, we would usually expect movement in a "positive" direction on the affective ties variable if affiliation occurs), and even the degree of congruence may change, as new group members come to understand and

TABLE 1
Relationship of Affective Ties with Group Members and Congruence of Group with Predispositions of Potential Converts

Congruence of group with predispositions of potential convert	Affective ties with members of group to which conversion is contemplated		
	Positive	Neutral	Negative
High	1	2	3
Medium	4	5	6
Low	7	8	9

accept a given group's beliefs and lifestyle. Thus, if a "non-affective" and/or "noncongruent" conversion does occur, then we would expect a "drift" toward cell one of the table for such individuals. Any movement counterdirectional to this tendency would be reason to expect eventual "deconversion" (a worthy subject for investigation itself—see Toch, 1965; Mauss, 1969; McHugh, 1970; Weiss, 1963).

A second comment relates to the first. The two major variables in the table are not independent of one another. Extant or developing affective ties may lead to more "congruence," just as initial congruence may contribute to the development of affective ties with group members.[10] Which variable usually has the strongest effect—and, thus, explains more conversions—is subject to some debate, as we have noted. Much more research needs to be done on this point, but we would suggest that one may have a stronger effect under certain circumstances, whereas the other will show more influence in yet others. For instance, total social isolates desiring affective ties (or just human interaction) may not attend to congruence factors as much as individuals with a strong (well-inculcated) commitment to certain beliefs (see Zygmunt, 1972: 460). It is theoretically possible, even predicted according to the Gerlach and Hine model, that individuals with high needs for affective ties (and possible other basic needs such as food and shelter) would convert to a group with which they had no basic "congruence." We found examples of both these extreme possibilities in conversions to Jesus movement groups, along with many other examples that fall somewhere between the extremes.

NOTES

1. The only claim of which we are aware for an explicit test is by Seggar and Kuntz (1972), whose study is itself open to serious questions. The "test" produced mixed results—which cannot be accepted as either vitiating or supporting the Lofland and Stark model.

2. The reason for selecting the Lofland and Stark model is that it is one of the most thorough available, combining predisposing and situation factors (or, in Zygmunt's, 1972, terms, incorporating motivational and interactional approaches) in one model. In the interest of space we will not present other models in detail here (see Richardson et al., 1977).

3. We do not deny that there are some problems in applying the individualism-collectivism dichotomy, and that in one sense it is a "false dichotomy." For instance, plainly some more or less conventional religious groups take different positions on a continuum with individualism and collectivism as polar types at either end, although most should probably be classified as closer to the individualistic end of the continuum. And it is just as plain that one would be foolish to classify all politically oriented solutions as collectivistic, for many (if not most) such solutions in our society involve a large dose of so-called "American individualism."

4. Exceptions to this conclusions are conceivable, as, for instance, when—as Toch (1965: ch. 8) says—someone joins a group with "latent reservations." If such a "conversion with reservations" was to a different orientation, then moving back to another orientation might be relatively easy. See Gordon (1974) for possible examples of this phenomenon.

5. We have used the phrase "groups and individuals" when talking about conversion to indicate that a more general model of conversion should incorporate "group conversion." There are some interesting, even classic, instances of *groups converting in mass* to new beliefs, as a result of circumstances affecting the entire group. Such instances, illustrated by the adoption of Christianity by entire tribes, families, or villages in India and Africa cannot be dismissed as shallow and meaningless for the individuals involved. Indeed, some of these "rice Christians" have been so "sincere" that their beliefs have been maintained through many generations in India (see the work of Sharma, 1968, in this regard). The circumstances surrounding the mass conversion usually involve severe deprivation of various kinds (see Glock, 1964, for a good discussion of types of deprivation), coupled with a strong legitimate authority structure. Given the tremendously rapid conversion of so many ex-drug devotees to the Jesus movement (and other movements), it is possible (and potentially theoretically fruitful) to build a case for something akin to group conversion occurring in recent American history.

6. Some may claim that including the notion of opportunity structure in predispositions is incorrect, and that it (and even "circumstances") should be more rightfully considered part of "situational factors." We disagree, and would further suggest that the dichotomous treatment of dispositions and situational factors by Lofland and Stark has been misinterpreted by some. Plainly, the dichotomy is meant only as an analytical device, for prior socialization affects one's view of "circumstances" or one's view of available "opportunities." Certain kinds of socialization generally preclude the interpretation of some circumstances as being frustrating, while other circumstances are felt to be intolerable *because of* the prior socialization (more on this later). And some "opportunities" are precluded by some world views, while yet others are seemingly obvious solutions to certain problems. Types of early socialization differ, not only in terms of content, but, perhaps as importantly, in terms of *methods used* in inculcating the content, and these differences have important implications. An interaction between types of early socialization and the experiences of life should not be unexpected.

7. The concept of "cognitive minority" is apropros here. Perhaps the best discussion of it in terms of this study is that of McGuire (1975), who develops the concept in her analysis of the Catholic neo-Pentecostal movement.

8. For more discussion of fundamentalism see also our earlier treatment (Richardson et al., 1972), in which we discuss fundamentalism as a form of what Lifton (1963) calls "religious totalism." Also, see our germane discussion of the "dependency-prone" personality type in Simmonds et al. (1976), and Simmonds' paper in this volume, which discusses an "addictive personality" type. And, since the Jesus movement is nearly completely glossolalic, see Richardson (1973).

9. Table 1 could be expanded to incorporate the point just made in the previous paragraph. As noted, our research demonstrates that what a person's significant others think of a group to which that person is considering affiliating is quite important in some cases, and that such considerations are of import in determining whether or not a person stays in a group once they have affiliated.

10. This same reasoning obtains in the obverse situation. Weakening affective ties may lead to less "congruence," and little initial congruence may preclude the development of meaningful affective ties.

REFERENCES

ADAMS, R. L. and R. FOX (1972) "Mainlining Jesus: the new trip." Society 9: 50-56.
DAVIS, R. and J. T. RICHARDSON (1976) "The organization and functioning of the Children of God." Soc. Analysis 37: 321-339.
ENROTH, R. M., E. E. ERICSON, and C. B. PETERS (1972) The Jesus People: Old Time Religion in the Age of Aquarius. Grand Rapids, MI: Eerdmans.
FROMM, E. (1950) Psychoanalysis and Religion. New Haven, CT: Yale Univ. Press.
GERLACH, L. and V. HINE (1970) People, Power and Change. Indianapolis: Bobbs-Merrill.
GLOCK, C. Y. (1964) "The role of deprivation in the origin and evolution of religious groups," in R. Lee and M. Marty (eds.) Religion and Social Conflict. New York: Oxford Univ. Press.
GORDON, D. (1974) "The Jesus people: an identity synthesis." Urban Life and Culture 3: 159-178.
HARDER, M. W. (1974) "Sex roles in the Jesus movement." Social Compass 21: 345-353.
———, J. T. RICHARDSON, and R. B. SIMMONDS (1976) "Life style: courtship, marriage and family in a changing Jesus movement organization." Int. Rev. of Modern Sociology 6: 155-172.
——— (1972) "The Jesus people." Psychology Today 6 (December): 45ff.
KIESLER, C. A. (1971) The Psychology of Commitment. New York: Academic Press.
LIFTON, R. J. (1963) Thought Reform and the Psychology of Totalism. New York: W. W. Norton.
LOFLAND, J. and R. STARK (1965) "Becoming a world-saver: a theory of conversion to a deviant perspective." Amer. Soc. Rev. 30: 862-874.
MARTIN, D. (1965) Pacifism: An Historical and Sociological Study. London: Routledge & Kegan Paul.
MAUSS, A. L. (1969) "Dimensions of religious defection." Rev. of Religious Research 10: 128-135.

McGUIRE, M. (1975) "Toward a sociological interpretation of the Catholic Pentecostal movement." Rev. of Religious Research 16: 94-104.

McHUGH, P. (1970) "Social disintegration as a requisite of resocialization," pp. 699-708 in G. P. Stone and M. Garverman (eds.) Social Psychology Through Symbolic Interaction. Waltham, MA: Ginn-Blaisdell.

PARRUCCI, D. J. (1968) "Religious conversions: a theory of deviant behavior." Soc. Analysis 29: 144-154.

PATTISON, E. M. (1974) "Ideological support for the marginal middle class: faith healing and glossolalia," pp. 418-455 in I. I. Zaretsky and M. P. Leone (eds.) Religious Movements in Contemporary America. Princeton, NJ: Princeton Univ. Press.

REIDY, M.V.T. and J. T. RICHARDSON (1977) "Neo-Pentecostalism in New Zealand." Forthcoming, Australian and New Zealand Journal of Sociology.

——— (1975) "Comparative studies of the neo-Pentecostal movement." Paper read at the biannual meeting of the International Conference for the Sociology of Religion, Spain.

RICHARDSON, J. T. (1977) "Types of conversion and 'conversion careers' in new religious movements." Paper read at annual meeting of the American Association for the Advancement of Science, Denver.

——— (1974) "The Jesus movement: an assessment." Listening: J. of Religion and Culture 9: 20-42.

——— (1973) "Psychological interpretations of glossolalia: a re-examination of research." J. for the Scientific Study of Religion 12: 199-207.

——— and M.V.T. REIDY (forthcoming) "Neo-Pentecostalism in Ireland." Social Studies: The Irish J. of Sociology.

——— (1976) "Comparison and contrast of two glossolalic movements." Paper read at annual meeting of the Society for the Scientific Study of Religion, Philadelphia, Pennsylvania.

RICHARDSON, J. T., R. B. SIMMONDS, and M. W. HARDER (1972) "Thought reform and the Jesus movement." Youth and Society 4: 185-200.

RICHARDSON, J. T., M. STEWART, and R. B. SIMMONDS (1977) Organized Miracles: A Sociological Study of a Fundamentalist, Youth, Communal Organization. (forthcoming)

SEGGAR, J. and P. KUNTZ (1972) "Conversion: evaluation of a step-like process for problem-solving." Rev. of Religious Research 13: 178-184.

SHARMA, S. L. (1968) "Comparative styles of conversion in major religions in India." J. of Social Research 11: 141-149.

SIMMONDS, R. B., J. T. RICHARDSON, and M. W. STEWART (1976) "A Jesus movement group: An adjective checklist assessment." Journal for the Scientific Study of Religion 15(4): 323-337.

——— (1974) "Organizational aspects of a Jesus movement community. Social Compass 21(3): 269-281.

TOCH, H. (1965) The Social Psychology of Social Movements.

TRAVISANO, R. (1970) "Alternation and conversion as qualitatively different transformations," pp. 594-606 in G. P. Stone and M. Garverman (eds.) Social Psychology Through Symbolic Interaction. Waltham, MA: Ginn-Blasidell.

WEISS, R. (1963) "Defection from social movements and subsequent recruitment to new movements." Sociometry 26: 1-20.

WHITE, R. H. (1968) "Toward a theory of religious influence." Pacific Soc. Rev. 11 (Spring): 23-28.

ZYGMUNT, J. F. (1972) "Movements and motives: some unresolved issues in the psychology of social movements." Human Relations 25: 449-467.

This UFO cult has been much in the news of late. Of special note in this paper is the very positive redefinition of the role of seeker. Also, the puzzling finding that affective ties between converts and group members seem unnecessary for coversion to occur is discussed, along with the similarly disconcerting idea that the group lacks ritual behavior.

Seekers and Saucers

The Role of the Cultic Milieu in Joining a UFO Cult

ROBERT W. BALCH
DAVID TAYLOR
University of Montana

During the early 1970s there was a resurgence of religious interest in the United States. Especially popular were the cults and sects which either drew their inspiration from non-Western religious traditions or rejected the moral relativism of the established Christian churches. Some of these groups, especially the Unified Family and the Children of God, grew so rapidly and transformed their members so completely that they were accused of "brainwashing" and "psychological kidnapping."

One of the most notorious cults captured national attention during the fall of 1975 when over 30 people suddenly disappeared in Oregon after attending a lecture about flying saucers. At the meeting, a middle-aged man and woman who called themselves Bo and Peep offered their audience eternal life in the "literal heavens." Bo and Peep—or the Two, as their followers called them—claimed to be members of the kingdom of heaven who had taken human bodies to help mankind overcome the human level of existence.[1]

ROBERT W. BALCH is Assistant Professor of Sociology at the University of Montana. His most recent research includes studies of rumor formation and jury selection. He was studying the sociological aspects of metaphysics and the occult in Arizona when he joined the UFO cult and he is working with David Taylor on a book about the cult.

DAVID TAYLOR is a graduate student in sociology at the University of Montana. His thesis is a participant-observer study of recruitment and conversion in the Unification Church.

Bo and Peep's prescription for salvation was rigorous. In order to enter the "next evolutionary kingdom," their followers had to abandon their friends, families, jobs, and material possessions. They traveled around the country in small "families," camping and generally leading a spartan existence. Bo and Peep told them they would be taken to heaven in UFOs if they could overcome all their human emotions and worldly attachments—a process they called Human Individual Metamorphosis. The name referred to a "chemical and biological change" that would transform their followers into new creatures with indestructible bodies.

Bo and Peep's UFO cult was one of the remarkable religious success stories of the mid-seventies. Within seven months after their first meeting in Los Angeles, the Two may have attracted as many as 150 followers.[2] The figure is noteworthy, because over 100 of them were recruited in just four meetings held in California, Oregon, and Colorado. The Oregon meeting is not only significant because of the national publicity it received, but because approximately 35 people decided to join afterwards. Most remarkable of all is that the Two rarely gave prospective members more than a week to make up their minds, and, when someone did, it was usually after less than six hours' contact with either the Two or any of their followers. The media speculated about brainwashing, and some ex-members got national coverage themselves when they accused the Two of "mind control." However, the accusation is not only sensational, but incorrect. In the following pages we argue that the decision to join Bo and Peep's UFO cult can only be understood in terms of the unique point of view of the metaphysical seeker, whose outlook is shaped by a religious underworld variously known as the cultic milieu (Campbell, 1972), the occult social world (Buckner, 1965), or the metaphysical subculture (Balch and Taylor, 1976b).

DATA COLLECTION

Shortly after Bo and Peep's Oregon meeting, we joined the UFO cult as hidden observers.[3] During the next seven weeks we traveled with several different families, observing and taking part in every aspect of their daily lives. Six months later we interviewed 31 ex-members in Arizona, California, Florida, Montana, and Oregon. Locating former members proved to be a difficult task, requiring extensive travel and a considerable amount of detective work. Using simple "snowball" sampling— each informant suggesting additional contacts—we eventually located 37 ex-members, six of whom preferred not to discuss their experiences. Although we did use an interview schedule, all interviews were informal and followed whatever format our respondents preferred. On the basis of the data we collected about cult members during the participant-observer phase of our study, we are confident that our sample is representative of the cult's membership.

Most members of the cult were in their early twenties, although their ages ranged from 14 to 58. There were roughly equal numbers of males and females when we joined, but, for reasons still unclear, a greater number of men was recruited during the time we observed the cult. A large minority had attended college, and the younger members were indistinguishable from college students anywhere in the United States. Their median occupational status was rather low, reflecting the cult's overall youthfulness and the fact that most members had changed jobs frequently, preferring not to be tied down to a routine that would limit their personal freedom.

SOCIAL ORGANIZATION OF
THE UFO CULT

The UFO cult was a loosely organized collection of seekers that depended on the charismatic appeal of Bo and Peep to hold it together. The Two and their followers traveled around the country holding public meetings to tell other seekers about their message. They moved every few days, camping out as they went. Encounters with the outside world were limited to a few highly structured situations. In order to survive, they asked for food, gasoline, and money at stores and churches, but their contact with outsiders was limited to asking for help. Only rarely did members explain who they were or mention Bo and Peep. Members also had contact with outsiders during public meetings. After the message had been presented, by either Bo and Peep or some of their followers, anyone in the audience could approach members of the cult to have his questions answered. However, the interaction was limited to discussing the message, and the answers given by members of the cult were often so stereotyped that they sounded like tape-recordings.

In order to speed up the metamorphic process, Bo and Peep assigned each of their followers a partner, usually a person of the opposite sex. The partnership was the basic unit of social organization. Its purpose was to develop "friction" and, ultimately, awareness of the human qualities each person had to overcome. Although partners were supposed to stay together 24 hours a day, sexual relationships and even friendships were discouraged. They were not only "too human," but they prevented the "friction" that would accelerate the metamorphosis.

Bo and Peep camped with their followers until a month after the Oregon meeting. Then, for reasons still unclear, they went into seclusion, explaining that they would return just before the spaceships came. They never set a date, however, and most of their followers never saw them again. Before they left, the Two divided the cult into several "families" of about 14 members each. Each family was headed by two spokesmen—a partnership appointed by Bo and Peep. However, their duties were never very well defined, and most members preferred a democratic arrangement where everyone had an equal voice. The spokesmen may have been appointed by the Two, but they were still earthly seekers like everyone else. Within a few weeks most spokesmen either had been replaced, or their position had been eliminated altogether.

Each family was completely autonomous, traveling almost constantly, going wherever it felt it was being led. Family members held public meetings of their own as they traveled. Most of them were small, but a few attracted audiences of several hundred people, and some of them were surprisingly successful, even without the charismatic presence of the Two. A meeting in northern Arizona produced nine new members, eight of them from a town with less than 500 people. Another meeting in

Berkeley, California, recruited as many as 20. But generally these meetings produced nothing more than catcalls and insults, or at best interested questions. During their random movements across the country, families rarely kept in touch with each other, and after the press lost interest in Bo and Peep's odyssey, many families had no way of learning anything about other members of the UFO cult.

Despite the importance of partnerships and families, the UFO cult was highly individualistic, a feature consistent with the individual nature of Bo and Peep's metamorphic process. Each member of the cult had to establish a direct psychic connection with a member of the next level, a process the Two called "tuning in." Bo and Peep instructed each of their followers to devote "100 per cent of his total energy" to "the process," which left no time for mundane activities like reading, singing, listening to the radio, or socializing with friends.

While traveling, the preferred arrangement was one partnership per vehicle, to prevent unnecessary social interaction. Although the rule was frequently violated, partners were expected to set up their camp away from other members of their family, and to keep to themselves except during family meetings. Aside from a brief period when members tuned in together before meetings, there was an absence of ritual in the UFO cult. Even this had its origins in Bo and Peep's desire to keep idle conversation to a minimum before meetings got underway. The Two even told their followers not to help each other with everyday jobs like fixing cars and putting up tents. They claimed that helping was not only an "energy drain" for the helper, but denied the person being helped an opportunity to confront and overcome his human nature—whether anger, frustration, fear, or overdependence on others.

Although we have referred to Bo and Peep's following as a cult, the group had a strong sectarian flavor (see Balch and Taylor, 1977). According to Wallis (1974, 1975a, 1975b), the fundamental criterion of the sect is "epistemological authoritarianism." Unlike the leaders of most cults, who recognize many equally valid paths to the top of the spiritual mountain, the Two claimed authoritative and privileged access to the Truth.

In a flyer they prepared for prospective members, Bo and Peep were quite specific about the uniqueness of their message:

> This is no spiritual, philosophic, or theoretical path to the top of the mountain. It is a *reality;* in fact it is the *only* way *off* the top of the mountain.

The cult's other sectarian features, e.g., its self-enforced separation from the world, make sense in light of the fact that Bo and Peep claimed to have the only path to true salvation.[4]

BECOMING A MEMBER OF THE UFO CULT

The recruitment process in the UFO cult was highly structured, and varied little even after Bo and Peep disappeared. If members felt that their connection at the next level wanted them to hold a meeting, they would find a suitable place and put up posters announcing the meeting, usually in "head shops," in health food stores, and around college campuses. After the Two disappeared, speakers for each meeting were selected by other members of the group. During the meeting itself they would be flanked by members of their family, who were called "buffers" because they absorbed the negative energy projected by hostile members of the audience.

The entire presentation generally took 15 or 20 minutes, but in one meeting we observed that the message was delivered in only three minutes. After a lengthy question-and-answer period, those who were sincerely interested in learning more about the message would be invited to a follow-up meeting, usually held in another place on the following day. These people would be asked to leave their names and phone numbers so that they could be contacted later that night. During the first meeting, the location of the follow-up would be kept secret to prevent curiosity seekers from showing up the next day. The follow-up meeting was usually more informal. The message would be restated, and the "prospective candidates" would have a chance to ask any additional questions that had not been answered the day before. At no time during our observations did we see members of the cult try to convince the audience using "hard-sell" tactics that Bo and Peep's message was true.

Within a few days of the follow-up meeting, those who were ready to join were told the location of a "buffer camp" where the socialization of new members would occur. Indoctrination in the buffer camp was very low-key, consisting of informal discussions around the campfire with Bo and Peep, and once in a while a private audience with them in their tent. After the Two disappeared, family spokesmen took over the job of socializing the new members, but the nature of the process remained the same. Rather than being subjected to intense social pressure and eventual demands for public commitment, new members were encouraged to spend as much time as they could alone with their partners, getting in tune with the next level. Interaction between new and old members was generally confined to informal discussions around the campfire, when the newcomers were encouraged to ask questions and express their doubts and anxieties. Some of these meetings were spent in almost complete silence, as members sat quietly around the fire tuning in, baking potatoes, or just watching the stars.

The most significant feature of Bo and Peep's recruitment strategy was the way it limited interaction between members of the cult and potential recruits. Virtually all such interaction was confined to stereotyped encounters at the two public meetings described above. When a prospective member decided to join, leaving behind his friends, family, and career, he did so on the basis of only a few hours of highly structured interaction with members of the group. Under these circumstances, new recruits almost never established close affective ties with members of the cult before they joined. Furthermore, during those two public meetings, the candidate learned very little about the cult's day-to-day existence. Since the Two believed that everyone had to decide on the basis of the message alone, they often refused to answer practical questions like "What do you eat?" and "Where do you get your money?"

Even after a seeker decided to join, he got very little social support from members of the cult. The buffer camp was usually located a day's drive away from the meeting place, and new members had to get there on their own as a test of their commitment. In one case prospective members were given four days to reach a post office 800 miles away, where they found directions to the buffer camp scribbled in the Zip Code book. Nine people decided to join that day, and all of them got to the camp on time and became members of the group.

The absence of affective ties with members of the cult is especially remarkable considering the importance of this factor in the sociological literature on recruitment and conversion. In their influential study of the "Divine Precepts" cult, Lofland and Stark (1965) argue that "cult affective bonds" are a necessary condition for joining. Yet Bo and Peep could recruit as many as 35 people at once without satisfying this condition.

Lofland and Stark (1965) distinguish between verbal and total converts, with verbal converts defined as those who profess belief and are accepted by core members, but take no active part in the everyday life of the cult. According to Lofland and Stark, "intensive interaction" is necessary to transform the verbal convert into a total convert, who is behaviorally as well as ideologically committed to the movement. They define intensive interaction as "concrete, daily, and even hourly accessibility" to other members which overcomes any remaining uncertainty about the truth of the cult's message (Lofland and Stark, 1965: 873).

Although becoming a member of a deviant religious group is usually seen as the end-product of a long process of social interaction, the entire process in the UFO cult was compressed into a few days. When new members arrived at the buffer camp, they had already made a substantial behavioral commitment to the cult. While some members had little to lose by joining, others left behind good jobs, homes, and even small children. Many new members began telling others about the message even before they reached the buffer camp. The zeal of these "instant converts" often exceeded the enthusiasm of the older members who greeted them at the campground.

We would not deny the importance of intensive interaction in strengthening the commitment of new members, but its role has been exaggerated. New members of the UFO cult were most likely to drop out during the first week after they joined, usually because of loneliness or their inability to cut themselves off from friends and relatives in the outside world. But the attrition rate for new members is high in most cults and sects, even those that do provide their fledgling recruits with strong social support (e.g., Zablocki, 1971).

THE SOCIAL WORLD OF THE
METAPHYSICAL SEEKER

We believe that social scientists have overemphasized the importance of cult affective bonds in recruiting new members, because of the dominant conception of the cult as a *deviant* religious organization. For example, Yinger (1970: 279) refers to cults as "religious mutants, extreme variations on the dominant themes by means of which men struggle with their problems." Because cults are deviant groups in a skeptical rationalistic society, many social scientists have assumed that the people who join them require a tremendous amount of social support to draw them in and insulate them from a hostile disbelieving world. However, if the seeker lives in a social milieu where the movement's assumptions make sense, and if he defines joining as the logical extension of his spiritual quest, then it is easy to understand how he could join a "deviant" religious cult without first establishing social ties with those who already belong. We will begin our discussion by characterizing the life style of Bo and Peep's followers before they joined the cult. Then we will explore the social world of the metaphysical seeker, showing how that style of life is an integral part of a cultic milieu where joining a cult is not only tolerated, but often encouraged.

THE PROTEAN STYLE
OF THE METAPHYSICAL SEEKER

In his discussion of the "protean man," Lifton (1970) describes the dilemmas confronting men and women in postindustrial society. In response to "historical dislocation" and the "flooding of imagery" produced by rapid change and mass communication,

Lifton argues that modern man has adopted a protean style, named for the Greek mythical figure, Proteus, who could change his form at will.

> The protean style of self-process is characterized by an interminable series of experiments and explorations—some shallow, some profound—each of which may be readily abandoned in favor of still new psychological quests. [Lifton, 1970: 319]

The description seems to fit members of the UFO cult very well, especially their "strong ideological hunger" (Lifton, 1970: 319) and pattern of shifting allegiances.

Before joining Bo and Peep, members of the UFO cult had organized their lives around the quest for truth. Most described themselves as spiritual seekers. After listing all her previous spiritual "trips," a woman who joined the cult when we did remarked: "Until I started talking to you, I never realized how much shit I'd been into." The woman, then 21, said she ran away from home at age 15 "to find the truth," and she had been searching ever since. An older member aptly characterized their perennial quest as a "bumper car ride through a maze of spiritual trips."

True to the protean style, most members of the cult moved frequently and had relatively few material possessions and social commitments. Their emotional ties with the conventional American style of life were generally weak. Hardly any of them had ever voted, and most of them were uninformed and unconcerned about contemporary social and political issues. A disproportionate number were remnants of the counterculture who preferred to avoid commitments that would unduly restrict their personal freedom. One man captured the protean flavor of his life when we asked him what he had given up to follow the Two:

> I gave up a lot to come on this trip, man. I gave up my record collection, a set of tools, my old lady. But it's not the first record collection I've given up, and it's not the first set of tools. And I've had eight old ladies.

Although a significant number of cult members had given up good jobs and comfortable homes to join the cult, most had not. For some of the younger members, the material aspects of life in the cult were not very different from what they had experienced before they joined. For example, one new member had just dropped out of the Christ Family, a small sect that wandered barefoot from town to town, begging for its food and lodging. For him the transition to Bo and Peep's nomadic UFO cult was easy. Many others had been traveling around the country with backpacks or in remodeled vans, rarely staying anywhere for more than a few weeks at a time.

Even those who made substantial material sacrifices to join were not strongly attached to their possessions. A member who joined after selling his house for five dollars explained: "For me it was easy. I'm single. I just had some property to which I never felt any attachment anyway." Some of those who appeared to have made the greatest sacrifice had been gradually divesting themselves of their material possessions long before they met the Two. In one instance publicized by the Oregon press, a middle-aged couple supposedly abandoned their house and family to join the cult. Actually one of their sons came with them, and, even before they ever heard of Bo and Peep, they had quit their jobs, sold their home, and moved into a commune, where they were living when they decided to join.

The protean style of Bo and Peep's followers is important, because weak attachments to extracult relationships and activities make one available for membership. Other things being equal, a man with a good job, a family, and a respectable position in the community is less likely to join a flying saucer cult than a single male living alone or in a commune, with few material possessions and a strong penchant for change and excitement. To a great extent, the reason is the different degree of social constraint in each person's life.

THE ROLE OF THE SEEKER
IN THE CULTIC MILIEU

Although the protean style fits most members of the UFO cult, we must avoid the trap of relating macroscopic structural conditions to the microscopic world of individuals without specifying the intermediate links in the causal chain. From

Lipton's description of the protean man, it would seem that individuals respond to the structural dislocations of our time as if they were social isolates, completely out of touch with other alienated members of our anomic society. However, alienation is a collective phenomenon. As Zygmunt (1972: 256) points out, men tend to become "alienated together."

Before they joined, members of the UFO cult shared a metaphysical world-view in which reincarnation, disincarnate spirits, psychic powers, lost continents, flying saucers, and ascended masters are taken for granted. This world-view, which Ellwood (1973) calls the "alternative reality," has a long history in the United States. It is perpetuated by a cultic milieu that exists in virtually every large community in the country. This milieu consists of a loosely integrated network of seekers who drift from one philosophy to another in search of metaphysical truth. We have entitled this section "The Role of the Seeker" because the concept of role places the individual seeker squarely in this social milieu. Within the metaphysical social world, the seeker is not disparaged as a starry-eyed social misfit. Instead, he is respected because he is trying to learn and grow. Members of the cultic milieu tend to be avid readers, continually exploring different metaphysical movements and philosophies (Buckner, 1965; Campbell, 1972; Mann, 1955). Whether in a tipi in the Oregon woods or a mansion in Beverly Hills, their evenings are often spent with friends and acquaintances discussing metaphysical topics like psychic research, flying saucers, or Sufi mysticism. A significant part of their lives is devoted to the pursuit of intellectual growth, however undisciplined that may be in conventional academic terms.

There is a common expression in metaphysical circles: "There are many paths to the top of the mountain." The seeker believes the quest for Truth is a highly individual process. As a long-time seeker in the UFO cult put it: "It looks to me like we're all trying to find the way. But what works for me, what's a test for me, may not mean shit to you." The long climb to the top of the mountain is usually a zig-zag course, as the seeker tries one path after another on the way up, always open to new ideas and alternatives.

Like Lifton's protean man, the seeker has a processual identity which changes continuously throughout his life. To stop exploring is to stop growing. Life is seen as an infinite series of "growth experiences," and the language of personal growth, like Christian's concept of humility, can be used to cope with almost any crisis. No matter how much he had given up to follow Bo and Peep, every one of the ex-members we interviewed defined his membership in the cult as a good growth experience. While a cynic might argue that this is nothing more than a convenient rationalization for a stupid mistake, it is clear that the quest for growth is part of the seeker's vocabulary of motives (Mills, 1940) that is learned and shared in the cultic milieu.

Many members of the UFO cult received strong support and encouragement from their friends when they considered joining the cult. Even many of those whose friends and relatives were very skeptical reported that no one tried to hold them back: "They told me, if that's what you feel you have to do, then you had better do it. It doesn't matter what we think."

Although it should be obvious, it is also worth noting that seekers get married, have children, and socialize their sons and daughters into the cultic milieu. As one member, whose mother was an avid follower of Edgar Cayce, told us, "I was raised on this stuff." The youngest member of the UFO cult was an extremely bright boy of 14 who had joined the cult with his parents. For over a year before hearing the message, he had read extensively about mysticism, psychic phenomena, health foods, and spiritual healing. He had been socialized into the occult social world, and the role of the seeker, even before he had the chance to experience the unsettling social dislocations described by Lifton.

The social nature of the alternative reality suggests that we need to reformulate the conventional image of the seeker. Our conception of the personally *disoriented* searcher "floundering about among religions" (Lofland and Stark, 1965: 869, 870) should be replaced with an image of one who is socially *oriented* to the quest for personal growth. Seekership constitutes a social identity that is positively valued by the individual and his significant others.

A closer look at the alternative reality of the metaphysical social world can help us understand how the Two could recruit so many followers in such a short time without providing prospective members with affective bonds to the group.

BO AND PEEP'S APPEAL
TO SUBCULTURAL VALUES

Although Bo and Peep's message sounded bizarre to practically everyone who read about it in the newspapers, it was firmly grounded in the metaphysical world-view. Bo and Peep put together an eclectic mixture of metaphysics and Christianity that many seekers found appealing because it integrated a variety of taken-for-granted beliefs, including flying saucers, reincarnation, Biblical revelations, and the physical resurrection of Jesus. (See Balch and Taylor, 1977, for a more complete explanation of the cult's belief system.) One of the Oregon recruits described his reaction to the message this way: "There were so many truths, man. I listened to Bo's rap, and I'm thinking, yeah, I've heard that before. He told me a lot of things I already knew, but he put them all together in a way I'd never thought of."

Despite its roots in the taken-for-granted beliefs of the cultic milieu, Bo and Peep's message had many unique features, e.g., the physical nature of the metamorphic process and role of UFOs in transcending the human level of existence. Yet, as Wallis (1974, 1975a, 1975b) points out, the cultic milieu is epistemologically individualistic, acknowledging many paths to spiritual enlightenment. In the metaphysical social world anything is possible. As one of our informants reminded us, it was not too long ago that Buck Rogers, spaceships, and ray guns were science fiction. Since then we have put men on the moon and sent a spaceship to Mars, and laser-beams are now being contemplated as military weapons. In a world that changes as rapidly as ours, he said, one cannot afford to close one's mind to any possibility, even spaceships from heaven. Not many seekers were completely convinced by the Two when they heard the message, and many remained skeptical as long as they belonged to the cult, but they set aside their doubts. Another ex-member captured the openness of the metaphysical seeker when he explained that the "willing suspension of disbelief" is an essential part of any genuine spiritual quest.

Although Bo and Peep claimed that their metamorphic process was the only way of getting to heaven, whenever they spoke to an audience they couched the absolutism of their message in language designed to appeal to the open-minded tolerance of the seeker. They agreed that there were many equally valid paths to the top of the mountain, but they added that only a UFO could get the seeker *off* the mountain into the kingdom of heaven that lies far beyond this planet.

In spite of the cult's sectarian characteristics, even Bo and Peep's "process" was a direct outgrowth of the epistemological individualism of the cultic milieu. The Two called their process Human Individual Metamorphosis to emphasize the uniqueness of each individual's transformation. The psychic connection established with the next level was unique for every member of the cult, and no two individuals had the same attachments to overcome. Nor would they require the same experiences to complete their metamorphosis. As members were so fond of saying: "The process is an individual thing."

Bo and Peep also appealed directly to the value of personal growth. It was a central part of their cosmology. According to the Two, Earth is only one of many "gardens" throughout the universe that supports life. All life forms are in a constant state of flux, evolving slowly but steadily to higher levels of consciousness. The Two compared Earth to a school, and mankind to its students. As human beings advance through a procession of lifetimes, they learn from their experiences, moving up through the grades from kindergarten to graduation time.

Bo and Peep said that by abandoning his past and making a connection with the next level, the seeker could accelerate his growth to the point where he would actually convert himself into an androgenous being. Even at the next level, there is no finality or perfection as there is in the Christian's heaven—only more growth. They said that not even God is perfect, because perfection means stagnation. As one member put it succinctly: "Growth is life."

THE SUBCULTURAL BASIS
OF THE MOTIVATION TO JOIN

The value placed on personal growth in the metaphysical social world helps account for the motivation to join the UFO cult. The prevailing image of the religious seeker is a social misfit who experiences one crisis after another before he finally joins a cult or a sect in order to cope with his problems. There is no doubt that most members of the UFO cult had experienced "psychic deprivation" (Glock, 1964) before they joined. In a typical account, a young woman described the spiritual vacuum of her life before Bo and Peep: "I could get high so many ways— drugs, music, scenery, people—but I still felt an emptiness. I never felt that fullness, that rock-bottom solidness I was looking for."

However, most social scientific studies of cults are overly reductionistic in their focus on the personal problems of cult members. They ignore the extent to which psychic deprivation is generated by the role of the seeker. One of Lofland and Stark's (1965) subjects aptly described the seeker's dilemma when she said: "The more I search, the more questions I have." The top of the spiritual mountain is an elusive goal, continually receding the higher the seeker climbs. The seeker is supposed to grow by asking for tests and learning from his experiences, but growth is subjective and hard to define. As one member explained: "You never know if you pass a test." In short, the motivation to continue searching is built into the role.

As the seeker goes through life, he is attuned to signs that might give his quest some direction. An axiom of the alternative reality is that nothing happens by pure coincidence. Things happen because they are meant to, and it is the seeker's job to ferret out the hidden meaning in everyday events that might reveal his role in the cosmic plan.

Most of the ex-members we interviewed reported a series of coincidences just before they joined which convinced them that Bo and Peep's message was true. Consider the case of a 22-year old woman who joined in a small Arizona community where she had been living for several months. She had been feeling restless and thought about moving on, but she had no particular destination in mind. Then one night during a violent thunderstorm, a lightning bolt suddenly lit up her room while she was asleep. As she sat up with a start, only half awake, she had a fleeting vision of an open doorway suspended in the air directly in front of her. At the time the meaning of the vision escaped her, but a week later she met two members of the UFO cult who told her about an open doorway in the heavens that would allow them to leave the planet aboard UFOs. The coincidence of her restlessness, the vision, and the sudden opportunity to join the UFO cult was compelling evidence that she was meant at least to take a closer look at Bo and Peep's message.

The seeker is understandably open to metaphysical teachers who might be able to clarify some of the confusion surrounding his spiritual quest and accelerate his growth. In the world of metaphysics there is a premium on hidden wisdom, whether Kabbalistic lore, tales of astral visits with ascended masters, or messages from benevolent space brothers. Metaphysics is the study of things beyond the realm of normal human experience, and the more obscure the hidden mysteries, the more the seeker needs a teacher.

Whether consciously or not, metaphysical teachers often maintain their authority by exploiting the seeker's insecurity. A skillful teacher can effectively suppress the open expression of doubt by implying that his students will comprehend his obscure metaphysical teachings according to their level of spiritual awareness. Like the villagers in the story of the emperor's new clothes, not many students are willing to risk revealing their ignorance by challenging a man they and their fellow seekers consider a master of the hidden mysteries.

Bo and Peep played on the insecurity of the seeker in much the same way. They compared their followers to twelfth graders who were about to "graduate from the planet" because they had evolved as far as they could in their present human form. Supposedly the rest of mankind was unable to understand their message because it was still plodding along through the other 11 grades.

THE ABSENCE OF CONVERSION
IN THE UFO CULT

Members of the UFO cult were not converts in the true sense of the word. Conversion, according to Travisano (1970: 600-601), refers to the "radical reorganization of identity, meaning, and life. . . . In conversion, a whole new world is entered, and the old world is transformed through reinterpretation. The father sees his bachelorhood as youthful fun; the convert sees his as debauchery." However, members of the UFO cult did not undergo a serious rupture of identity when they became "total converts" to Bo and Peep's message. Instead, they defined "the process" as a logical extension of their spiritual quest.

Unlike members of more sectarian organizations such as some Jesus movement group who define their lives before "accepting Christ" in very negative terms (Richardson et al., 1972), Bo and Peep's followers tended to look favorably on their pasts. The following remark is typical: "This information clarified everything we had been into before. It's like the next logical step."

The continuity between participation in the UFO cult and the role of the seeker in the cultic milieu stood out most clearly when members became disillusioned with the process and considered dropping out. Their disillusionment was accompanied by discernible changes in their everyday speech. Many words, phrases, and conversational topics unique to the UFO cult began to disappear from their talk. They stopped talking about UFOs and the physical nature of the metamorphic process, and began to emphasize how they had grown from their experience in the cult.

In a manner consistent with the protean style, most ex-members of the UFO cult insisted that Bo and Peep, however misguided they appeared in retrospect, had accelerated their spiritual growth by helping them overcome their mundane attachments:

> The most important thing is the process of becoming. Don't get hung up on the future. Just let it be. It doesn't matter what you call it—the process is the path, the way, the Tao. All the great teachers were saying the same thing—Jesus, Lao Tzu, Buddha, the Two. . . . The process is whatever you want it to be as long as you're free of attachments.

Paradoxically, the openness that allowed so many seekers to suspend their doubts and follow the Two also facilitated the process of dropping out. For example, one ex-member recalled something his partner told him just before he decided to leave the cult:

> He said over and over again just before I left the trip: "We have to keep an open mind about this thing, man. The Two may not be who they say they are, but that's not important. The Two aren't important."

His comment is significant for two reasons. First, it illustrates the seeker's protean adaptability. It was fairly common for members to argue, just before they left the cult, that Bo and Peep were no longer important. The Two had merely brought them some useful information, and now that they had learned all they could from the process, it was time to move on, to overcome even their attachment to Bo and Peep. Second, his comment reflects the common belief that even a charlatan may have something to offer. A reporter once asked a member what he would think if Bo and Peep's message turned out to be a hoax. "Then I will still have grown," he replied.

For most of Bo and Peep's followers, then, becoming a member of the UFO cult did not constitute the rejection of one identity for another. Instead, their decision to follow the Two was a *reaffirmation* of their seekership. Whenever one identity grows naturally out of another, causing little disruption in the lives of those involved, the term "conversion" is inappropriate. Perhaps prospective members of a religious cult only need strong social support from existing members when a radical substitution of belief systems is required.

CONCLUSION

While there is no way of knowing how successful Bo and Peep would have been with different recruitment methods, it is clear that the absence of social interaction between members and would-be recruits is not necessarily a fatal omission in recruiting members to a contemporary religious movement. However deviant it might appear to the outside world, a religious cult is not necessarily deviant within the social world of the metaphysical seeker. Even if it were, there are powerful norms that encourage an open-minded assessment of deviant beliefs and discourage condemning others for doing what they think is best for themselves. When a religious seeker also has few social commitments and material possessions, most of the major restraints against joining a deviant religious cult are absent. To a great extent, even the motivation to join such a group is generated by social-psychological forces operating in the cultic milieu.

The curious pattern of recruitment in Bo and Peep's UFO cult underscores the importance of studying religious cults in their social and cultural context. The process of becoming a member may vary greatly depending on the social milieu from which a cult draws its members, and the extent to which membership requires a transformation of one's social identity in that milieu.

NOTES

1. Before their "awakening," the Two apparently led rather ordinary lives. Bo, who was 44 at the time of the Oregon meeting, had been a music professor at a university in Texas, and later a choir director for an Episcopal church. Peep, 48, had been a professional nurse. After meeting in a Texas hospital in 1972, they opened a short-lived metaphysical center specializing in astrology, spiritual healing, theosophy, and comparative religions, where they first began to suspect their higher purpose on the planet. During the next three years they spent much of their time traveling together, deliberately isolating themselves from the rest of the world in order to learn more about their mission. It was not until the spring of 1975 that they recruited their first followers at a private meeting in Los Angeles.

2. Estimating the size of Bo and Peep's following at any given time is hazardous, because members were scattered across the country in small families, and no one, not even the Two, kept track of the number of people recruited. While estimates of the cult's size at the peak of its popularity range up to 1,500, there were probably never more than 200 members, and 150 is probably more realistic. These figures are based on our own calculations as well as estimates made by members themselves.

3. Although we were aware of the ethical objections to covert observation, we decided to join the cult as hidden observers for pragmatic and methodological reasons. Pragmatically there was no other way to study the cult effectively, because although members spoke freely with reporters, they generally limited their comments to the "party line" dictated by the Two. We believed the only way we could get accurate data about the cult

was to join it ourselves. Our judgment was supported by the sharp contrast we observed between daily life in the cult and the way members presented themselves to the outside world (Balch and Taylor, 1976a).

The pragmatic considerations that led to our joining as hidden observers dovetailed nicely with our ethnographic methodological orientation. As Barkun (1974: 43) points out in his recent study of millenarian movements, research that offers an "inside" perspective is all too rare in the study of religious cults. The works of Festinger et al. (1956) and Lofland and Stark (1965; Lofland, 1966) are conspicuous exceptions. They are notable not only because they are unusual, but because of the significant contributions they have made to the study of religious movements.

In addition to allowing us to enter the "backstage region" of the cult (Goffman, 1959), we believed our decision to join as hidden observers would enable us to see the world through the eyes of Bo and Peep's followers as no other method could. Several months later, when we more openly interviewed members who had dropped out of the cult, our "inside" knowledge of the group's beliefs, organization, and membership helped us focus our questions and contributed to the excellent rapport we enjoyed with our respondents. As one ex-member said of another social scientist who had tried unsuccessfully to study the cult: "He didn't even know what questions to ask."

It is worth noting that we encountered no hostility when we revealed our "true" identities prior to each interview, and no one refused to be interviewed because of the deception. In fact, we were asked to contribute a chapter to a book about the cult that is being written by several ex-members.

4. At this writing the UFO cult still exists, and its sectarian features are more pronounced than ever before. Bo and Peep rejoined the remnants of their following sometime during the early months of 1976. Since their return, the cult has stopped recruiting and has become very secretive, disappearing almost entirely from the public view. These changes are described in Balch and Taylor (1977).

REFERENCES

BALCH, R. W. and D. TAYLOR (1977) "The metamorphosis of a UFO cult: a study of organizational change." Paper read at the annual meeting of the Pacific Sociological Association, Sacramento, California.

—— (1976a) "Salvation in a UFO." Psychology Today 10: 58-66, 106.

—— (1976b) "Walking out the door of your life: becoming a member of a contemporary UFO cult." Paper read at the annual meeting of the Pacific Sociological Association, San Diego, California.

BARKUN, M. (1974) Disaster and the Millennium. New Haven, CT: Yale Univ. Press.

BUCKNER, H. T. (1965) "The flying saucerians: an open door cult," pp. 223-230 in M. Truzzi (ed.) Sociology and Everyday Life. Englewood Cliffs, NJ: Prentice-Hall.

CAMPBELL, C. (1972) "The cult, the cultic milieu, and secularization," pp. 119-136 in M. Hill (ed.) A Sociological Yearbook of Religion in Britain, Vol. 5. London: SCM Press.

ELLWOOD, R. S., Jr. (1973) Religious and Spiritual Groups in Modern America. Englewood Cliffs, NJ: Prentice-Hall.

FESTINGER, L., H. W. RIECKEN, and S. SCHACHTER (1956) When Prophecy Fails. Minneapolis: Univ. of Minnesota.

GLOCK, C. Y. (1964) "The role of deprivation in the origin and evolution of religious groups," pp. 24-36 in R. Lee and M. E. Marty (eds.) Religion and Social Conflict. New York: Oxford Univ. Press.

GOFFMAN, E. (1959) Presentation of Self in Everyday Life. Garden City, NY: Doubleday.

LIFTON, R. J. (1970) "Protean man," pp. 311-331 in R. J. Lifton (ed.) History and Human Survival. New York: Random House.

LOFLAND, J. (1966) Doomsday Cult. Englewood Cliffs, NJ: Prentice-Hall.

——— and R. STARK (1965) "Becoming a world-saver: a theory of conversion to a deviant perspective." Amer. Soc. Rev. 30: 862-875.

MANN, W. E. (1955) Sect, Cult and Church in Alberta. Toronto: Univ. of Toronto Press.

MILLS, C. W. (1940) "Situated actions and vocabularies of motive." Amer. Soc. Rev. 5: 904-913.

RICHARDSON, J. T., R. B. SIMMONDS, and M. W. HARDER (1972) "Thought reform and the Jesus movement." Youth and Society 4: 185-200.

TRAVISANO, R. V. (1970) "Alternation and conversion as qualitatively different transformations," pp. 594-606 in G. P. Stone and H. A. Farberman (eds.) Social Psychology Through Symbolic Interaction. Waltham, MA: Xerox.

WALLIS, R. (1975a) "Scientology: therapeutic cult to religious sect." Sociology 9: 89-100.

——— (1975b) "The cult and its transformation," pp. 35-49 in R. Wallis (ed.) Sectarianism. New York: John Wiley.

——— (1974) "Ideology, authority, and the development of cultic movements." Social Research 41: 299-327.

YINGER, J. M. (1970) The Scientific Study of Religion. New York: Macmillan.

ZABLOCKI, B. (1971) The Joyful Community. Baltimore, MD: Penguin.

ZYGMUNT, J. F. (1972) "Movements and motives: some unresolved issues in the psychology of social movements." Human Relations 25: 449-467.

The eastern mystical tradition's movement into American life is depicted in this paper, which reports on the intriguing pattern of changing attitudes toward the use of psychotherapy among many members of the two major groups studied and also suggests a new rationale to justify psychotherapy.

Patients and Pilgrims
Changing Attitudes Toward Psychotherapy of Converts to Eastern Mysticism

DICK ANTHONY
University of North Carolina, Chapel Hill

THOMAS ROBBINS
Queens College, City University of New York

MADELINE DOUCAS
THOMAS E. CURTIS
University of North Carolina, Chapel Hill

At present there seems to be a heightened spiritual ferment involving the emergence of novel religious and quasi-religious movements. The therapeutic function of these movements in providing alternatives to conventional psychotherapy and models for new therapies has been widely noted (Zaretsky and Leone, 1974; Marin, 1975; Lasch, 1976; Schur, 1976).[1] Many of the new movements affirm a "monistic" symbolic universe associated with oriental mysticism (Anthony and Robbins,

Authors' Note: *This research was supported by Public Health Service Grant Number 5-R01-DA00107 05.*

DICK ANTHONY is a Research Associate in the Department of Psychiatry at the University of North Carolina at Chapel Hill. He has for several years been coinvestigator of an interdisciplinary research project studying new religious movements.

THOMAS ROBBINS is Assistant Professor of Sociology at Queens College, City University of New York. He has been engaged in a long-term investigation of some new religious movements and has published several papers of note in recent years, many of them coauthored with other members of the research team.

MADELINE DOUCAS is a member of an interdisciplinary research team studying new religious movements at the Department of Psychiatry, University of North Carolina at Chapel Hill. She is interested in investigating interactions between religious and psychotherapeutic orientations.

THOMAS E. CURTIS, M.D., is Professor and Chairman of the Department of Psychiatry, School of Medicine, University of North Carolina at Chapel Hill. For the past four years he has collaborated with Dick Anthony and Thomas Robbins on a long-term study of the effects of counter-culture religions on problems of identity in youth.

[65]

1975) The link between Americanized "eastern" mystical currents and contemporary therapies associated with the "Human Potential Movement" has also been noted (Braden, 1967; Back, 1973; Marin, 1975; Anthony and Robbins, 1976). Beyond these relationships, one eminent sociologist of religion has noted the convergence of Hindu-Buddhist mysticism with the underlying "neomystical" attitude of contemporary psychotherapy which "looks for salvation within the putative depths of human consciousness itself" (Berger, 1970: 89).

This paper describes the experiences with psychotherapy of converts to the Meher Baba and Guru Maharaj-ji movements. These groups are prominent examples of the new eastern movements in America. Extensive participant observation among both "Jesus movement" and eastern groups has convinced us that the latter are more likely than Jesus groups to recruit from people who have had some experience with psychotherapy. The incidence of experience with psychotherapy also seems higher among eastern converts than among the general public. The reasons for this correlation seem to involve the greater likelihood of eastern converts' exposure to background factors which would predispose them to involvement with psychotherapy.

Glock (1972, 1976) has argued that traditional individualistic and theistic modes of accounting for social causality are incompatible with the deterministic tendencies within social science. Glock and Piazza (1975: 21) write:

> More and more people are learning about Freud, Marx, Jung, Keynes, their popularizers, and about psychoanalysis, psychology, sociology and other social sciences. This means, we suspect, that more people are structuring reality from the perspective of the social modes and fewer are doing so according to the individualistic and supernaturalistic modes.

Presumably, acculturation to the social scientific mode of "reality structuring" would predispose people to involvement in psychotherapy. Glock and Piazza found that such acculturation was greater than average among people who were younger, better educated, and more liberal politically. Wuthnow (forthcoming) has found that people who participate in eastern religious movements (yoga, zen, or Transcendental Meditation) also tend to be better educated, more intellectually sophisticated, and more politically liberal. Elsewhere (Wuthnow, 1967a: 280), he found that people who are attracted to such movements are more likely to "value spending time to know your inner self" and to be "high on subjective discontent" (1976a: 290). Presumably these factors would also predispose people toward involvement in psychotherapy.

In an additional study, Wuthnow (1976b) found that although mystical and social scientific meaning systems can be distinguished from each other, they often converge into a perspective he labels "modern." He (1976b: 126-127) argues that such convergence results because:

> [The mystic] operates . . . within a matrix of sensory and symbolic conditions that determine his ability to construct reality. These conditions are not entirely self-imposed; to an important extent they are socially imposed, which gives mysticism a certain resemblance to social science. The important assumption, however, is that one need not be limited by the reality in which he lives, for by simply perceiving it differently, he can change it.

Apparently, psychotherapy—as a form of applied social science—and eastern mysticism involve assumptions which are rather similar. Such similarities may lead some people to regard psychotherapy and mysticism as *alternative* methods of changing reality by changing their perceptions of it.

Followers of Meher Baba and of Guru Maharaj-ji appear to go through a sequence of stages with respect to their attitudes toward psychotherapy. Converts to both movements have often had experience with psychotherapy prior to their spiritual involvement. In fact, disillusionment with orthodox psychotherapy may partially stimulate their interest in these movements. Upon conversion, members of both movements tend to see further involvement with psychotherapy as superfluous. However, many members of the Meher Baba movement eventually come to see selective use of psychotherapy as complementary to achieving spirituality. This latter trend toward harmonizing religious and psychotherapeutic involvement is not as well developed in the Guru Maharaj-ji movement. However, the Guru Maharaj-ji movement is a newer movement, and there are some indications that its members will also evolve in this direction.

The factors underlying this sequence of attitudes toward psychotherapy reflect basic trends in American culture. The explication of these trends illuminates a current value crisis in psychotherapy. A problem of orthodox psychotherapy is its dependence on the *medical model*. The medical model has functioned to reconcile the patient's feelings of helplessness and powerlessness with the dominant ethos of personal autonomy and responsibility. Orthodox psychiatry confers the *sick role* on the patient, thus designating him as a *special case* and converting his "sickness" into an implicit affirmation of the autonomy and mastery of "nonsick" responsible citizens. In this way the medical model implicitly upholds the "Protestant ethic" of mastery and personal responsibility (Davis, 1938).

It is precisely this ethic which is increasingly undermined by the seemingly "impersonal" social processes of an urbanized and bureaucratic "mass society." As mentioned above, the popularization of deterministic scientific and social scientific notions also has eroded assumptions of unconditional responsibility for personal behavior and social outcomes (Glock, 1972, 1976). The anchorage of the medical model in the disintegrating Protestant ethic thus constitutes a liability for traditional psychotherapy. Particularly vulnerable to criticism are the crucial assumptions that "sick" persons are *atypical* and that "nonsick" persons are masterful and autonomous. This assumption fits a situation in which very few persons seek psychotherapeutic assistance. It is difficult to square with a situation in which a significant proportion of the middle class seek such assistance. Are such persons all "sick"? Is a pathological self-concept appropriate for all outpatients seeking counseling when a vast majority are holding down responsible instrumental roles? In short, the medical model, with its central device of the "sick" role, seems incompatible with the contemporary routinization of psychotherapy as a conventional life process. The medical model cannot adequately legitimate the *normalization* of psychotherapy.

Our concern with these issues has arisen as a result of observing the fluctuating relationship between monistic-spiritual and psychotherapeutic perspectives among followers of Meher Baba and Guru Maharaj-ji. We have been studying the Meher Baba movement for ten years and have analyzed various aspects of the movement in several papers (Robbins, 1969; Robbins and Anthony, 1972; Anthony and Robbins, 1974). Our ongoing study of the Baba movement has been based on extensive participant observation and numerous taped interviews.[2] We have observed the Guru Maharaj-ji movement less intensively over the last five years. We have described elsewhere the convergence of its meaning system with the monistic orientation of Baba followers (Anthony and Robbins, 1975). (A complementary description of the Guru Maharaj-ji movement has been published by Messer, 1976).

STAGE ONE:
PRECONVERSION EXPERIENCES WITH
PSYCHOTHERAPY

As mentioned, devotees of "eastern" movements have often been involved in psychotherapy prior to conversion to a mystical perspective. Our subjects, like most seekers of private therapeutic assistance, did not go to psychiatrists because they were unambiguously "sick." Rather, they had found it difficult in the contemporary technocracy to live up to exaggerated expectations of mastery and autonomy intrinsic to the traditional Protestant ethic. This difficulty often produced identity confusion and apathy which elicited concern from others. The excerpt below, in which a Baba-lover discusses her malaise prior to therapy, is typical of a number of passages in our interview protocols:

> I was spending my time that I wasn't working in bed with my shades drawn, either reading or just plain drowning in my mind or something like that. I was just like totally bubbled and bemuddled and I didn't want to get out of it either. . . . And so my parents encouraged me to go to my family doctor.

Nonpsychotic psychiatric patients have frequently had difficulty operationalizing the traditional ethic of mastery. In a sense, their problem is really social and *ideological,* i.e., a lack of an ethic congruent with pervasive social experiences. Nevertheless, the medical model of orthodox psychiatry may initially appeal to such patients, because the sick role is *extenuating.* It shields them from Protestant ethic demands and provides a deterministic explanation for wayward actions and experiences (e.g., "early childhood influences or unconscious forces makes me the way I am"). However, the cost of this insulation is a "sick" self-concept or "sick" concept of significant others who may have influenced one's development. This is not always functional for daily living. A "sick" explanatory model can also seem demanding to the individual, despite the insulation it grants. The subject quoted above comments:

> I really felt a stigma of having to be treated for something. . . . I got to the point where I could seek the help but I was ashamed or embarrassed to tell other people that I was seeing somebody for therapy, because they would think that there was something wrong with me.

A "sick" model may also appear in time to the patient as an inadequate or even repressive conceptualization of one's tensions with the social milieu. A Guru Maharaj-ji follower states:

> What I was discovering was that a lot of my insecurities and a lot of the problems and things that I felt about myself weren't necessarily because I was maladjusted. A lot of the problems I had had as much to do with the culture I was living with as they had to do with myself. . . . I felt that [psychiatrists] were showing people, like, interact within a basically sick society. How to get along. And like I wanted more than that.

The "sick" self-concept also has a tendency to become *self-fulfilling* and may hinder the eventual development of a sense of competence and autonomy.

An additional problem of medical model psychotherapy is its impersonal conception of the therapist's role. Within this model, the therapist is seen as a doctor who is administering "technical" expertise. Young persons seeking therapeutic assistance are often seeking surrogate parents, identity figures, and role-models. The professional role-orientation of the psychiatrist may frustrate these needs. One Baba-lover recalls:

> [The therapist] never said much and he seemed to me kind of "out to lunch." And one day as I was leaving he said, "Would you please tell your parents to pay the bill?" And there was something in the way that he said it. . . . Here was this guy who didn't give a flying fuck about my existence, you know, who was just interested in . . . and was pretty bored with what the hell I had been saying. It really hurt me. It really turned me off and I never went back.

Finally, some subjects were concerned that orthodox psychotherapy does not effectively embed insights in a meaningful "overview" or general conceptualization of the universe. Today, "A secular-minded psychoanalysis now encounters everywhere among its patients a sense of meaninglessness against which it is helpless" (Barrett, 1976: 37). A Guru Maharaj-ji follower recalled:

> I never could get a handle on therapy. I never could somehow get the hang of being in a therapeutic situation . . . all my life I always when I wanted to understand something, like I've always wanted to get an overview of something . . . and something about the therapy group and a lot of the literature I read, it seemed superficial because there was something there I wasn't understanding.

STAGE TWO:
SPIRITUAL AWAKENING—
THE HONEYMOON PERIOD

Contemporary problems of meaning involve the failure of traditional overarching systems of meaning—e.g., the Protestant ethic—to provide a coherent interpretation of experience in a technocracy. Alternative meaning systems, such as those of the Meher Baba or Guru Maharaj-ji movements, involve a transformation—at a very general level of organization—of the system by which individuals interpret their intrapsychic and interpersonal experience. We have described elsewhere how conversion to mystical movements can ameliorate contemporary problems of meaning. In general, our analyses have described how such involvement alleviates communal deprivation (Anthony and Robbins, 1974) and moral confusion (Anthony and Robbins, 1975). In this section we shall touch upon those aspects of the transformation of converts' interpretative procedures which affect their attitudes toward psychotherapy.

Usually, our subjects perceived psychotherapy as unnecessary during an initial period after conversion to a mystical perspective. In part this was because their conversion to a mystical movement involved *assimilation to a community*. Since many of the problems which initially led them to seek therapy involved the vicissitudes of interpersonal relationships, their assimilation to a "loving" spiritual community dissolved some of these problems. A follower of Guru Maharaj-ji recalled her initial meeting with other devotees:

> I immediately felt a rapport with the people, you know. And it was incredible, because they could look at me right in the eye. They were totally unafraid to look you right in the eye, smile at you, and extend love to you. And they were talking about the way I wanted to be living. They were connected to the truth and they were connected to God in a totally groovy way.

As mentioned above, moral confusion in a technocracy is also a contributing factor to contemporary problems of meaning. The concept of *Karma*—which is a prominent feature of the mystical theodicies of our subjects—has been interpreted so as to partially alleviate such confusion for our subjects. A Guru Maharaj-ji follower stated:

> But one thing I experienced, or I don't experience anymore, when I get into these things is that I don't experience guilt. There's no sense of guilt involved. And, again, it's like, you know, if I do something inconsistent with knowledge, it's you know, I know it's my *Karma*. And probably there's something I'm learning from it. And I definitely consciously have the experience of later on realizing what I am supposed to learn from the experience.

What is particularly interesting from our standpoint is the interpretation of Karma, or the deterministic law of retribution across incarnations, as a *therapeutic learning process*. Another Guru Maharaj-ji follower comments:

> Okay, my view is that if a person's poor, he's poor because there are lessons for him to learn in being poor. And that the end result of all these lessons would be that he'll realize God. Possibly not in this life-time, but eventually. It's not so much he's being punished for being bad, but that the situation is actually a good learning situation. Because there's just something that your soul has to learn.

Thus, the notion of Karma, as interpreted by many of our subjects, involves a sort of naturally occurring alternative to psychotherapy built into the fabric of the universe. Karma is not interpreted as mechanistic moral retribution, but as a *spiritual learning process* associated with the soul's quest for monistic realization and self-insight. Within the monistic theodicy of our subjects, the goal of such learning is the eventual experience of the unity of all existence. This goal is summed up in Meher Baba's phrase, "We are all one." Below, a Guru Maharaj-ji follower discusses the realization of the oneness of the universe and the divine potential of one's "real self":

> When you're stuck in this place of like viewing the world through your own limited concepts and your limited mind, your view of the world is just too narrow. It's just so narrow. When you even begin to get beyond that, the whole universe opens up. And it's like I'm realizing that the reason that there is suffering in this world is because of two things—ignorance and selfishness, or really just one thing, because selfishness comes from ignorance. And the ignorance is just being ignorant of your real self, you know. And our real self is like God, our real identity, you know, pure, pure consciousness. But, what Maharaj-ji is doing is showing people a way to experience their own divinity, to experience their own truth, their own true self. And once you have the tiniest experience of that it's just everything, it just changes your whole perspective.

For a variety of reasons then, new converts to eastern groups experience their spiritual involvement as a path to self-insight and self-improvement, which renders conventional therapy superfluous. As one follower of Guru Maharaj-ji recalled:

> Well I was getting into knowledge [spiritual experience] and I was like coming to the therapy group and talking about Guru Maharaj-ji and knowledge . . . and I was, well, actually I was so blown away by *Satsang* [testimonial ritual] that I sort of freaked out, you know. I had a contract with my therapist that I had to go a number of times. And like I wanted to, I didn't want to do my contract, because I felt I was getting it from this *Satsang.*

In general, our subjects' spiritual involvement superceded psychotherapy because it offered an *integrated* cosmological and moral framework which psychotherapy had not. A follower of Meher Baba remembered:

> I felt like, I have Baba now, so I don't need therapy now. It made me feel whole. It gave me a goal and a direction. I stopped feeling I was crazy. I felt that coming to Baba gave me a sense that I had a moral scheme. I had a sense of values . . . I sort of remember [thinking], "I don't remember therapy being at all helpful in making me feel more stable and that I could get a handle on what I was doing to myself."

Thus, rejection of formal psychotherapy is a frequent concomitant of conversion to mystical groups. One respondent noted, "There are really a lot of spiritual aspirants who think psychology is a lot of crap." The perceived obsolescence of psychotherapy may be associated with a rejection of the intellect as a basis for problem solving. The "analytic" character of traditional psychotherapy is often seen as irrelevant to "real growth," which must have an "experiential" basis.[3] One follower of Guru Maharaj-ji told an interviewer:

> I mean you can counsel and you can go to psychiatrists. You can try and talk out the problems of the inhibitions you have or the problems or the trauma that you deal with. But, on one level, that's just like, just an intellectual kind of help. You try to keep joyous thoughts in your mind. But, the thing is, you're still

thinking. It might be very difficult for someone to understand unless having the *experience* of meditation. It's an experience where the mind stops, where thought ceases and . . . pure experience takes place. [emphasis added]

Another aspect of conversion to a mystical movement which may contribute to alienation from formal therapy is the acceptance of the spiritual master as a sort of cosmic therapist. Converts believe that their spiritual master manipulates their experiences so as to aid them in their quest for self-insight. A Baba-lover recalls her first few years of following Meher Baba:

It was very intense with Baba and I was, like, I was feeling a lot of development. I was feeling a lot of internal development. And my life changed radically. I was going through a lot of new experiences and I was feeling growth occurring and I felt Baba's hand very strongly guiding all of these events in my life. So I felt that I was, I doubt if I would have called it under therapy, but I was under the hand of a master, and I was living a spiritual life. There was a purpose to everything that was happening. . . . So, and I felt like problems were being worked out.

A relationship with a master is seen as producing awareness which is superior to that produced by formal therapeutic relationships, because a master speaks from knowledge rather than opinion. A follower of Guru Maharaj-ji commented:

I'll never forget that because I can really feel now that Guru Maharaj-ji, and by that I mean the truest and most steadfast guide I have found to this point said, you know, spoke very clearly . . . I said that to myself, "I want *the* best Guru. I want *the* Guru who knows," you know.

Secular psychology is seen as an imperfect derivative of the ultimate knowledge possessed by the master. A Baba-lover comments:

I think . . . when I came to Baba, it made therapy seem very archaic. I mean psychology . . . as a very archaic science, a very, not "archaic," that's the wrong word, *embryonic* science, you know, like shit, Baba was way beyond this, this science. These people were just beginning to get into it. Baba had gone way on through on to the other side.

Moreover, insights resulting from the master's guidance are not experienced as demeaning because they are accompanied by "unconditional positive regard." A Baba-lover comments:

> I always felt being with Baba made me feel that I have a potential in me and being in therapy with her [her therapist] anyway, or where I was at, made me feel that I was this nothing, just a total piece of shit and she was withholding all this judgment on me. And it just gave me this feeling that I had the power—that was the thing that impressed me most about Baba.

Such "judgmental" overtones in conventional therapy tend to reinforce negative self-concepts which originated in familial interaction. Spiritual masters, on the other hand, are usually depicted as quintessentially "loving." As such, they may be experienced as more effective parental surrogates than professional psychiatrists. A Baba-lover comments:

> [My mother] would always send out a double message of love and hate. "I love you. You're shit." Okay, and hearing about Baba, like this man was like spewing love, you know, just love without the "no, no, no, you know you're shit." Without the "you're shit" part.

Thus, relationships with conventional therapists often seem to have an invidious aspect. In contrast, relationships with Gurus or spiritual masters usually entail assumptions of the immanence of universal consciousness or divinity in the spiritual aspirant. Monism redefines life as a process of growth in which individuals awaken gradually from the "illusion" of separate ego-life. Awareness of such a process does not confer a stigma of unusual pathology. Involvement in mystical groups may thus be seen as involving *nonjudgmental* cosmic therapy.

Most of the features described so far as characteristic of mystical involvement remain relatively constant within the aspirant's spiritual evolution—although they are later reinterpreted as being compatible with some forms of psychotherapy. However, the early stages of involvement in a mystical movement may also involve unrealistic expectations of rapid spiritual apotheosis, e.g., Nirvana, Satori, God Realization. Such decisive realization could be expected to obviate all emotional difficulties. A Baba-lover recalls:

> It seemed like it would have an end to it. There was some final goal that Baba offered, okay, and that goal was a way out of the cycles that I was really tired. And it was a way of achieving some permanent state that would be satisfying and fulfilling. So that's what I was concerned with at first, with getting on the planes and getting through it and getting out of it.[4]

Related to eschatological expectations is the expectation of *ego-loss*. Emotional and interpersonal problems pertain to the (ultimately illusory) ego, and will naturally dissolve with the "dissolution of the ego." A Guru Maharaj-ji follower comments:

> But now my ego is something . . . to view as just excess baggage. I don't need it, and I don't want it, and it gets in my way.

The press of worldly experience tends to result eventually in the diminution of the unrealistic character of such expectations. Over time, converts realize that conversion to a mystical perspective does not result in the early transcendence of all earthly burdens. When such realization occurs, therapy sometimes reappears as an option for dealing with selectively problematic aspects of existence.

STAGE THREE:
REENTRY INTO PSYCHOTHERAPY

As we have seen, converts to mystical movements affirm monistic notions which help to relativize or extinguish problems. However, elevated expectations often develop regarding the efficacy of spiritual involvement in smoothing one's way in life. These expectations cannot always be fulfilled. Inevitably, it becomes apparent that conflicts, hang-ups, frustrations, and shattered relationships continue to emerge despite new spiritual insights. Devotees explain these developments in various ways. Some believe that the master "speeds up your Karma," i.e., the devotee must expect to have *more* hang-ups and hassles than the average person (or than they had previously) because he is making faster spiritual progress. The master is viewed as deliberately putting his "lovers" through the wringer. He is seen as intensifying stress in order to force the spiritual aspirant to examine feelings and perceive their derivation from the tricks of the separative ego. Such difficulties—properly dealt with— abridge the aspirant's spiritual journey by "working off" accumulated Karma.[5] The following dialogue between one of the authors and a Baba-lover illustrates this conviction:

> *Interviewer:* if all these hassles [breakup of marriages] occur afterwards what good is [becoming a Baba-lover], you know?
>
> *Respondent:* Well, my feeling on a long term basis is, who knows? What would have happened to these people without Baba. . . . I don't think that people who get into Baba get out of anything. I think they get into it but I think it comes out a lot faster. I think they have the same problems that they would have during a normal lifetime but I think the problems come out quicker and faster. To me, in reading Baba, it seems that the function of a master, you know, is not to work outside, you know, of the way a human being works, but to, you know, subconscious to conscious, quicker than normal.

In this connection, "posthoneymoon" Baba-lovers who have followed Meher Baba for several years are likely to reject notions of an immediate enlightenment and a short-term realization of the immanent oneness of the universe. The Baba-lover quoted above also commented:

> I don't think you just become free overnight and I'm very down on spiritual teachers who come around saying "Okay I'll give you grace tomorrow." . . . I don't think that's the way it works, you know. I think Baba's been very specific and explicit in explaining that I'm not going to get you out of the Karma that you've made up for yourself, but I'll help you work it out quicker.

Thus, the ultimate goal of "God Realization" and pure monistic enlightenment loses its immediacy and is assigned to a more distant future.

To devotees in this stage, the master is perceived as enmeshing them in problems for a therapeutic purpose; to take advantage of the opportunities for spiritual growth which lie hidden in these difficulties one must try to cope with problems *on the human level at which they manifest.* One cannot evade one's problems through occult sensations or resolve difficulties abstractly through monistic dogma. In short, one is not supposed to use the master as a crutch.

Once this stage has been reached, psychotherapy reemerges as a viable option in one's quest for self-insight. Therapy is a tool which the spiritual aspirant can use to probe his own feelings. Another Baba-lover comments:

> I felt . . . like I was consciously trying to modify my outward behavior in the world. And that kind of dropped away and I realized that I had all of these feelings and emotions that had been sat upon that have to come out. And I had to accept that as a part of me also, and I can't just go around doing this superficial behavior pattern that I think conforms to what Baba wants me to be like. I've got to, like, explore my own hunches. And that is why therapy is very important to me.

There is, thus, a tendency for some Baba-lovers eventually to *return to psychotherapy.* Those who do tend to comprehend the return to psychotherapy in spiritual terms.[6] The resumption of therapy is perceived as in line with Baba's purposes for his lovers and, thus, compatible with their overriding spiritual commitment. A Baba-lover comments:

> I see therapy as the thing that I need for a time just to help me see more clearly Baba in everything. And I need it now. I need that objective kind of time space to help me be able to see that . . . the way I look at [it] is, okay, fine, this therapy will end sometime and I'll go through another space of time where I don't need therapy to learn more, where Baba will give me different experiences in order to know more that Baba is everything and I'm Baba . . . maybe there'll be another time when I'll come back to a space where I'll need therapy again to help me focus more on . . .

Baba, you know, and everything. But that it's a tool, it's Baba's tool, and since I'm with Baba, he uses it when I need it and he won't when I don't.

Meher Baba is now perceived as a metapsychologist, rather than as embodying an incompatible alternative to psychotherapy. For Baba-lovers who return to therapy, Baba is now seen to *work through the formal therapy situation.* Meher Baba's thought and discourses with regard to spiritual awakening, dissolution of the ego, Karma, and *Maya* are now seen not as an incompatible alternative to psychology, but as an overarching *metapsychology* within which particular therapeutic processes and particular psychological concepts can be located. The following comment by a Baba-lover illustrates this attitude:

[Therapy] increases your compassion and understanding of people, and, . . . I am beginning to see myself and I hear people . . . explain what Jung says or what . . . Rogers or any other, like, really well-known people that I would read in psychology, what they say is just a different way of saying what Baba says in the *Discourses.*

Another Baba-lover comments:

as you get further into something like Baba, you begin to realize that, you know, science and psychology and bioenergetics all fit in, they're put in the proper order. . . . I don't see anything wrong with Freudian psychology or Skinnerian psychology or Jungian psychology or . . . Adlerian psychology except that if you look back into eastern literature, . . . you see that he's [Baba's] taken them all and put them in a, you know, in a very homogeneous context where everything has its place. And, if you read *The Upanishads* you'll find Skinner there, or *The Bhagavad Gita,* you'll find Freud in there and you'll find Jung in there and you'll find Adler in there too. But you'll find them all in a very . . . in a homogeneous . . . all fitting into a certain, you know, area kind of thing, here we've kind of . . . it's our trip in the west to compartmentalize things.

The respondent quoted above implies that Meher Baba's thought derives psychological insights from a general spiritual perspective which governs the total universe. Such insights, then, are not compartmentalized as insights into "pathology." Elsewhere in his interview protocol, the same respondent argues that Baba's conception of a universe which is essentially *consciousness* entails a continuous process of consciousness expansion, which converges with psychotherapeutic notions and can acclimate the Baba-lover to therapy. With a mystical value orientation, the devotee ceases to expect an immediate or short-range "cure" for his "pathology" and is reconciled to a continuous process of "growth" through an endless quest for self-insight:

> if you got a rational mind, you're supposed to use it, and to me, finally using it when you come into, you know, spirituality context, concepts of devil and heaven and hell and, you know, immediate salvation, do not fit in with what we know to be real.

Many members of these groups thus perceive a mutual reinforcement between therapy and mysticism. Their spiritual involvement actually enables them to get more out of therapy than they could formerly. A Baba-lover notes:

> It amazes me all the time, everytime it happens it amazes me, you know, but people really get better [in therapy] . . . I understand what's happening better than I ever have. I perceive [that] the kinds of things that people go through . . . they need to go through. The other thing is, I think, that's given me a greater faith in the realm of psychology, which is a very intangible world, you know, you can't touch it or anything . . . is being on the spiritual path and learning about mysticism, which is very intangible.

In other words, the determinism ("the things that people go through . . . they need to go through") and the "intangible" subjectivism of mysticism and monistic thought are seen to converge with presuppositions of psychotherapy as a "normal" life process.

It is interesting that the detached role-orientation of the professional therapist, which had been resented by our subjects in the past, is now sometimes perceived as valuable. Conceivably, one's needs for a parental surrogate or identity figure may be satisfied by a spiritual master. Thus, certain kinds of expectations are removed from the therapeutic situation. Moreover, many Baba-lovers themselves ultimately become psychotherapists or go into quasi-therapeutic counseling vocations (e.g., teaching disturbed children; Robbins and Anthony, 1972). Some of these subjects noted that the grounding of their psychotherapeutic orientations within a general metapsychological spiritual perspective has helped them become more effective therapists, by enabling them to become more detached from the results of their actions. A Baba-lover psychotherapist comments:

> Baba has helped me to understand, you know, that if you really are trying to help people as best you know how and trying to "serve humanity" or Baba-in-humanity or however you want to take it, you've really got to . . . do what you honestly feel is right and that may mean at times saying, you know, "look, man, you know, I think you're all fucking up, you know . . ." *I can see my detachment from my work develop with Baba* . . . it's just been a very subtle influence . . . I've slowly but surely become detached . . . and I think that's important, because Baba says, you know, even in his *Discourses* . . . he says . . . even the idea of, you know, helping others or of selflessness is a dispersed form of ego, you know, it's still *you* wanting to help other people.

In addition, when all human interaction is regarded as a form of cosmically directed therapy, psychotherapy *per se* ceases to be a special case involving imputations of deviance. Such a perspective frees clients of stigmas associated with pathological status. This perspective also frees the therapist from a need to *hide* behind an impersonal professional role. He is free to relate to clients more directly, without cloaking such interaction in the mystification of professional expertise. A Baba-lover psychotherapist comments:

> Since I've become a Baba-lover I've become a more honest and open person, less frightened of revealing myself, cause I have always been very defensive. And that's helped me in my therapy with people because certain patients you just have to, especially the sick ones, you have to be honest with them. And you have to set a good example that you're not frightened yourself, not that

you spill your guts out, but there are things that you want to talk about and say to realize about yourself.

The "detachment" which is developed by both therapists and clients within this perspective does not reinforce the resumption of the sick role by patients or the role of all-knowing expert by therapists. This sort of detachment, rather, encourages the mutual subordination of the perceptions and expectations of both therapists and clients to supervening spiritual orientations.

It appears that in "stage three" some of the same notions which initially rationalized an estrangement from therapy—notions of the spiritual master as a master psychologist and cosmic therapist, deterministic conceptions of Karma and notions of Maya and the illusory quality of ego dynamics—*now appear to legitimate a resumption of psychotherapy.* There is clearly a shift over time in the way in which these concepts are interpreted. It is our view that these notions, which posit a universe in which consciousness has priority over material reality, are intrinsically supportive of psychotherapy as a mode of coping with the vicissitudes of life. Monistic spiritual notions do not, however, support the traditional medical model of psychotherapy as well as they do growth-oriented and transpersonal models. When members of mystical groups resume therapy, they tend to gravitate toward growth-oriented and transpersonal therapies (e.g., Jungian therapy, Psychosynthesis, Polarity therapy, Gestalt therapy). While "eastern" mysticism may legitimate therapy, it may also contribute to the ongoing debunking of *traditional* psychotherapy and the increasing disassociation of psychotherapy from the medical profession.

Baba-lovers in "stage three" tend to see convergence between psychotherapies based on the "growth" model and Meher Baba's teachings. The question arises as to whether devotees of Guru Maharaj-ji will follow the path of Baba-lovers and also embark upon "stage three." Guru Maharaj-ji followers are generally younger than Baba-lovers and have usually been involved in their movement for a shorter time. On this basis one might expect them to evolve in the direction of Baba-lovers. On the other hand, the Guru Maharaj-ji movement is somewhat more totalistic and more communally tightly knit than the Meher Baba movement.

Moreover, it has structured rituals such as *Satsang* (testimonial ritual) which reinforce the feeling that the *knowledge* gained via meditation constitutes a self-sufficient response to problems of meaning for the devotee. The availability of an experiential technique—"The Knowledge"—which can reliably "*bliss out*" devotees may reduce the appeal of alternative therapeutic techniques. Nevertheless, we have seen indications that some followers are evolving toward what we have termed the "stage three" pattern of Baba-lovers. Below, one of the researchers relates the transformation he observed in a devotee over a two-year period:

> When I knew _____ two years ago, she was starry-eyed. Every-thing she did was related to Guru Maharaj-ji and meditation. She expected a radical transformation in her consciousness. She expected to be a dramatically different person in short order. Two years later, I saw her working at some job. She doesn't have that starry-eyed look. She seems more cynical. I asked her if she was still with Guru Maharaj-ji. She is, but meditation apparently isn't changing some parts of her personality and interpersonal rhythms. She is now going to Polarity Therapy. She feels optimistic about it. She doesn't see it as inconsistent with being a follower of Guru Maharaj-ji. She feels meditation and therapy do different things for her.

CONCLUSION

As we have seen, a psychotherapy tied to the medical model and, through it, to the "Protestant ethic" was perceived as inadequate and alienating by our subjects, who sought meaning and commitment in mystical movements. However, our subjects experienced disillusionment with too direct and simplistic a dependence on their spiritual involvements to resolve all difficulties immediately. Many of our informants now participate in various forms of psychotherapy, which they perceive as complementary to their overriding spiritual involvement.

It is our contention that the "monistic" symbolic universe of eastern mysticism converges with some of the assumptions of modern psychotherapy. Such a convergence provides an effective legitimation of psychotherapy, obviates the medical model, and grounds psychotherapy in a social milieu in which exaggerated assumptions of personal mastery and autonomous fate control have lost plausibility. The central interrelated elements of "monism" are (1) the ultimate metaphysical unity or "oneness" of all reality, (2) the ultimately illusory or nonobjective nature of the world (Maya), (3) the ultimately illusory nature of "separative" individuated ego-life, and (4) the importance of a quest for self-insight to enable one to dispel the illusion of separative ego-life, which is assumed to be the true source of all unhappiness and strife. Notions of reincarnation and Karma (the law of inevitable moral retribution operating across incarnations) are also salient elements of classical monistic systems.

The monistic model of reality in a sense *universalizes sickness;* everyone is "sick" in the sense that everyone who has not perfected his consciousness is subject to the conflicts and frustrations which inevitably afflict those imprisoned in separative ego-life. But if practically everybody is "sick," then nobody is really "sick" or pathological qua aberrant or abnormal in the process of seeking therapy. In a sense, everyone is aberrant from the norm of perfect monistic consciousness and, thus, in need of some sort of "consciousness expansion." Yet nobody remains as a pathological special case; *therapy is liberated from the medical model.*

Of course, many religious models might tend to universalize and normalize "sickness" as a fundamental human condition (e.g., "sin" in the dualistic Christian symbolic universe). It would appear, however, that the "monistic" world-view has certain advantages vis-à-vis traditional dualistic perspectives with regard to the legitimation and normalization of psychotherapy in the present environment. *Deterministic* elements in monistic philosophies (e.g., the influence of Karma from past lifetimes or the inevitable helplessness and powerlessness of those with undeveloped consciousness) may seem more meaningful than traditional voluntaristic perspectives in the context of urban social processes. Moreover, they converge to a degree with deterministic elements in psychotherapy, e.g., determination of present feelings by unconscious forces reflecting early childhood experiences. Second, *relativistic* elements in monism (the illusory status of "the world," the ultimate universal "oneness" which dissolves all moral polarities, the ultimate relativity of moral evaluations to the underlying development of consciousness in the actor) appear to "fit" the ongoing dissolution of traditional absolutistic morality in an increasingly "permissive" culture. They thus converge to some degree with the qualified moral relativism of psychotherapeutic perspectives in which growth of consciousness qua transcending neurotic complexes is a goal pursued at the expense of authoritarian moral codes. Finally, monism envisions a world which is essentially *consciousness*. Experiences are determined by one's underlying state of consciousness, and moral judgments must be relative to the actor's state of consciousness. In such a universe, "therapy" qua transcending of limitations of consciousness becomes the essence of salvation and a continuous and universal life process. Monistic spiritual awakening is not instantaneous and discrete qua being "born-again" or "baptized in the spirit"; it is a continuous evolutionary "growth." Formal psychotherapy may conceivably be interpreted as an aspect of this evolutionary spiritual process.

Our study provides evidence that mystical perspectives provide more effective orienting frameworks for psychotherapy than does the traditional Protestant ethic. Rieff (1966), in *The Triumph of the Therapeutic,* has argued that traditional psychotherapy has played a large role in undermining traditional religious perspectives. He furthermore argues that in some respects psychology has become the religion of certain segments of the population.

In Freud's (1971) work, the rivalry of psychoanalysis and traditional religion was explicit. The groundwork was laid, then—as psychoanalysis became dominant in psychiatry and gained immense cultural influence—for psychotherapy to replace traditional religion as a way of systematizing ultimate concerns. However, as psychotherapy has gained influence as a protoreligious system, its defects with respect to this role have become apparent. Consequently, some authors (Suzuki et al., 1963; Frank, 1961) have pointed out parallels and convergences between some forms of therapy and some types of religion. Other theorists (Maslow, 1964; Laing, 1967) have attempted to reformulate psychology as a sort of metareligion. Furthermore, modern theologians (Tillich, 1952) have attempted to rework traditional Christian theology so as to provide grounds for accommodation between psychology and some forms of religion.

The undermining of traditional religion by psychology appears to have been partly responsible for the emergence of new religious and quasi-religious therapeutic movements. Some of these movements, most notably mystical movements of eastern origin, escape many of the criticisms leveled by psychology against traditional religion. Other movements—e.g., *est*, Scientology—provide a synthesis of psychology and religion.

The increasing popularity of mystical and quasi-mystical therapeutic movements has resulted in a variety of criticisms. Schur (1976) has argued that such movements reflect increasing privatism and a retreat from political responsibility. In a somewhat similar vein, Marin (1975) has argued that such movements are popular because they offer rationalizations for inequitable social privileges. Lasch (1976) has extended these arguments into the psychotherapeutic realm. He contends that the increasing popularity of mystical and quasi-therapeutic religious movements are a reflection of the widespread increase of the psychiatric syndrome of "narcissism." He feels that such movements exacerbate the syndrome—although they may offer temporary symptomatic relief.

On the other hand, this study would tend to indicate that, for our subjects at least, mystical involvement has resulted in a decrease rather than an increase of the symptoms of narcissism. Our subjects' involvement in these movements has resulted in an increase in their capacity for (1) impulse control, (2) ability to sustain long-term committed relationships, (3) responsible vocational involvements.

A partial explanation for these contradictory observations may lie in the fact that Schur, Marin, and Lasch all have built their arguments on rather casual observations rather than longitudinal studies of the movements they purport to be describing. Their arguments also seem to be colored by an anchorage in a traditional "dualistic" perspective which has become increasingly untenable in contemporary social circumstances. Such a perspective assumes that what Weber called "inner-worldly asceticism" is the only viable basis for an ethic of social responsibility. Robertson (1975), however, has argued that such an orientation is simply untenable in a "late capitalist" society. Attempts to maintain such a perspective in contemporary America will simply result in increasing social disorganization and anomie. Robertson argues, furthermore, that social responsibility in contemporary circumstances must be anchored within a religious perspective he refers to as "ascetic mysticism." This perspective is similar to one we have earlier described as characteristic of the Meher Baba movement (Robbins and Anthony, 1972; Anthony and Robbins, 1974).

Finally, the opposition between Schur, Marin, and Lasch, on the one hand, and Robertson and ourselves, on the other, may partially result because we are comparing apples and pears. Marin and company have tended to focus on movements of American origin—e.g., *est*—which are syntheses of explicitly psychotherapeutic perspectives with rather vague mystical notions. We, on the other hand, have tended to focus on explicitly mystical movements of eastern origin. Such movements bear a complementary relationship to growth-oriented psychotherapy—as we have demonstrated in this paper. However, their somewhat more complex mystical orientations of a traditional eastern sort may save them from some of the liabilities alluded to by these other authors.

Perhaps the clearest implication of this study is that further research needs to be done on the relative social and psychological assets and liabilities of different sorts of mystical and quasi-mystical therapeutic movements. We have made a tentative stab in this direction by developing a four-cell typology of mystical movements (Anthony and Robbins, 1976). Within this somewhat speculative study we attempt to assess the differential implications for personal and social integration of involvement in different sorts of mystical movements.

NOTES

1. Zaretsky and Leone (1974) have suggested that the present upsurge of noninstitutionalized religious and quasi-religious movements can be explained in part in terms of a need to develop do-it-yourself alternatives to professional services in areas such as psychotherapy or child-rearing. Professional social services are increasingly provided at prohibitive cost, as well as in an impersonal manner.

2. Authors Anthony and Doucas have themselves been followers of Meher Baba since the late 1960s, while Robbins has been considerably influenced by the movement.

3. This orientation can be derived from the basic assumptions of monism. If everything is "oneness" and the phenomenal world is illusory, then the categories which make possible analytical thought are ultimately illusory and will be resolved into undifferentiated cosmic oneness. Seeking to experience monistic oneness takes precedence over the exploration of illusory polarities, which conceal the underlying unity of experience (Anthony and Robbins, 1975).

4. "The plane" apparently refers to higher planes of consciousness.

5. Although Meher Baba is seen as manipulating one's circumstances, this is thought of essentially as facing the devotee with challenges. How the Baba-lover responds is supposed to determine spiritual progress and future Karma. In this way, the Baba-lover gains a sense of responsibility for his own situation in the context of Karmic determinism.

6. Becoming involved in psychotherapy subsequent to conversion is a common but by no means universal tendency among Baba-lovers. Recently, one of the authors attended a Baba meeting at which several followers were discussing their recent experiences in therapy. Several other Baba-lovers objected to discussion of psychotherapy at Baba meetings. It became apparent, however, that the latter did not object to Baba-lovers having psychotherapy, but felt that there were other matters which they would rather hear discussed at Baba meetings. It also became aparent that most of those present had at some time been involved in therapy and had found such involvement useful.

REFERENCES

ANTHONY, D. and T. ROBBINS (1976) "A typology of non-traditional movements in modern America." Paper presented at the annual convention of the American Association for the Advancement of Science, Denver.

——— (1975) "Youth culture spiritual ferment and the confusion of moral meanings." Paper presented to the Society for the Scientific Study of Religion, Milwaukee. Also in J. Douglas (ed.) Deviant Subcultures (forthcoming). New York: Little, Brown.

——— (1974) "The Meher Baba movement: its effect on post-adolescent social alienation," pp. 479-511 in I. Zaretsky and M. Leone (eds.) Religious Movements in Contemporary America. Princeton, NJ: Princeton Univ. Press.

BACK, K. (1973) Beyond Words: The Story of the Human Potential Movement. Baltimore, MD: Penguin.

BARRETT, W. (1976) "On returning to religion." Commentary 62 (November): 33-38.

BERGER, P. (1970) A Rumour of Angels. New York: Anchor.

BRADEN, W. (1967) The Private Sea: LSD and the Search for God. Chicago: Quadrangle.

DAVIS, K. (1938) "Mental hygiene and the class structure." Psychiatry 1: 55-65.
FRANK, J. D. (1961) Persuasion and Hearing: A Comparative Study of Psychotherapy. Baltimore, MD: Johns Hopkins Univ. Press.
FREUD, S. (1971) The Future of an Illusion. New York: Doubleday, Anchor.
GLOCK, C. (1976) "Consciousness among contemporary youth: an interpretation," pp. 353-366 in C. Glock and R. Bellah (eds.) The New Religious Consciousness. Berkeley: Univ. of California Press.
——— (1972) "Images of 'God,' images of man and the organization of social life." J. for the Scientific Study of Religion 11 (March): 1-15.
——— and T. PIAZZA (1975) "Explorations into the structuring of reality." Paper presented at the annual Meetings for the Scientific Study of Religion. Available in the Working Paper Series of the Survey Research Center, University of California at Berkeley.
LAING, R. D. (1967) The Politics of Experience. New York: Pantheon.
LASCH, C. (1976) "The narcissist society." New York Rev. of Books (September 30): 5-12.
MARIN, P. (1975) "The new narcissism: the trouble with the human potential movement." Harpers 251 (October): 45-56.
MASLOW, A. H. (1964) Religions, Values and Peak-Experiences. Columbus: Ohio State Univ. Press.
MESSER, J. (1976) "Guru Maharaj Ji and the Divine Light Mission," pp. 52-72 in C. Glock and R. Bellah (eds.) The New Religious Consciousness. Berkeley: Univ. of California Press.
RIEFF, P. (1966) The Triumph of the Therapeutic: Uses of Faith after Freud. New York: Harper & Row.
ROBBINS, T. (1969) "Eastern mysticism and the resocialization of drug users: the Meher Baba cult." J. for the Scientific Study of Religion 8 (Fall): 308-317.
——— and D. ANTHONY (1972) "Getting straight with Meher Baba: a study of drug-rehabilitation, mysticism and post-adolescent role conflict." J. for the Scientific Study of Religion 11 (June): 122-140.
ROBERTSON, R. (1975) "On the analysis of mysticism: pre-Weberian, Weberian, and post-Weberian perspectives." Soc. Analysis 36: 241-266.
SCHUR, E. (1976) The Awareness Trap: Self-Absorption Instead of Social Change. Chicago: Quadrangle.
STONE, D. (1976) "The human potential movement," pp. 93-115 in C. Glock and R. Bellah (eds.) The New Religious Consciousness. Berkeley: Univ. of California Press.
SUZUKI, D. F., E. FROMM, and R. De MARTINO (1963) Zen Buddhism and Psycho-analysis. New York: Evergreen.
TILLICH, P. (1952) The Courage to Be. New Haven, CT, and London: Yale Univ. Press.
WUTHNOW, R. (forthcoming) Experimentation in American Religion. Berkeley: Univ. of California Press.
——— (1976a) "The new religions in social context," pp. 267-293 in C. Glock and R. Bellah (eds.) The New Religious Consciousness. Berkeley: Univ. of California Press.
——— (1976b) The Consciousness Reformation. Berkeley: Univ. of California Press.
ZARETSKY, I. and M. LEONE (1974) Religious Movements in Contemporary America. Princeton, NJ: Princeton Univ. Press.

A part of the "occult establishment" is described in this paper, along with the presentation of a model whereby "normal people" get involved in an occult group. A discussion of the importance of group ritual in such a process is included.

Toward a Theory of Conversion and Commitment to the Occult

FREDERICK R. LYNCH
Pitzer College

In an article published in 1970, Marty observed that an "Occult Establishment" had emerged in the 1960s, a phenomenon for which social scientists seem totally unprepared.The Occult Establishment was so named by Marty because it had emerged as the vehicle for a "respectable" middle-class revival of interest in heretofore "deviant" or "far out" occult topics such as reincarnation, extrasensory perception, psychokinesis, witchcraft, astrology, and other unseen energies, forces, and laws at work within the "hidden order" of the occult. At about the same time, other sociologists began to take note of and attempt to classify and analyze the multifaceted occult renaissance (see especially Truzzi, 1972, 1974a, 1974; Tiryakian, 1973, 1974; Zaretsky and Leone, 1974; Eliade, 1976), as did writers outside the social sciences (cf. Holzer, 1972, 1973, 1974; Freedland, 1972; Godwin, 1972; Greenfield, 1975; Webb, 1974; Wilson, 1973).

Apart from Marty's (1970) suggestion that the occult is now middle-class and "respectable," why has there been a revival of

---

FREDERICK R. LYNCH has been on the faculty of Pitzer College of the Claremont Colleges since 1973. His areas of research and teaching interests include sociological theory, social change, sociology of the supernatural, and field methods.

interest in the occult? According to Truzzi (1972), the modern occult is part of popular culture, a sort of "pop religion." This very popularization has served to demystify beliefs and practices which were once regarded with fear and awe. Staude (cited in Tiryakian, 1973) views youth's interest in the occult as a search for meaning similar to the religious and cultural renewal of the renaissance. This rendering is also highly congruent with a much more sarcastic description of a "Third Great Awakening" by satirist Wolfe (1976). Greeley (1970) feels that the occult revival represents a renewed search for community and "groupism."

At best, though, these portrayals of the occult revival are merely loose descriptions offering suggestions for more empirical studies. Except for studies by Scott (1976) and Balch and Taylor (1976), the processes whereby people take up and maintain involvement in the occult have remained almost as "hidden" as the cosmic laws occultists seek to understand and utilize. Indeed, the most recently published survey of "new religious movements," edited by Glock and Bellah (1976), completely ignores the Western occult tradition of witchcraft and paganism.

It is my intention in this paper to construct a descriptive framework for studying conversion and commitment to the occult. The effort is grounded in an ethnographic study of an occult organization which I shall call the Church of the Sun. A description of this organization, a summary of the members' social characteristics, and the factors which led to their initial and continued involvement in the Church of the Sun follow a brief presentation of methodology.

METHODOLOGY

I first made contact with the Church of the Sun by enrolling in a six-week course on "basic wicca" in the summer of 1975, a class which was taught at an occult supply shop in a metropolitan area in California. The shop was owned and partially operated by the founder of the Church of the Sun, his wife, and a somewhat younger partner who had also become the second-in-command in the church. The latter taught the course on Wednesday evenings, when the shop was closed to the public. At the end of the course, and after I had expressed a continued interest in the occult, I was given a signed invitation card to attend a "Saturday Night Service" at the Church of the Sun, a major weekly affair which was open to members and invited nonmembers. These services usually attracted from 30 to 45 persons per week.

For three months, the "Professor from＿＿University," as I was known by some (I have deleted the institutional affiliation in order to provide greater anonymity), attended and partici- pated in these services, which offered a variety of lectures, meditation exercises, hypnosis demonstrations, and full-blown magical rituals, the latter purportedly drawn from the traditions of ancient civilizations and the oral occult tradition. Also, from time to time, I participated in brief, postsession social gatherings. I wrote up detailed observations immediately after each of these gatherings.

The members and guests who came to know me were aware that I was both personally and professionally interested in their group and in the occult, and that I was currently engaged in teaching a university-level course on the social and historical contexts of paranormal belief systems. Some of the members and I occasionally discussed in an off-hand manner the possibility of my studying the Church of the Sun. While most expressed polite or good-humored interest, no one seemed to care particularly one way or the other.

As the church embarked upon a fateful reorganization in early January, I approached Harold Hall (a pseudonym), the leader, with the idea of my studying the organization for the purpose of charting its history as well as finding out what kinds of people join his church—or "Lodge," as it is now called—why they do so, and why they remain or quit. He seemed quite intrigued with the idea. He agreed to be interviewed himself and to let me interview other members. And we both heartily agreed upon my continuing as a participant-observer so that I might reflexively grasp the meaning of their work, how they made sense of themselves and the universe through the utilization of occult beliefs and techniques. (On methods of field research and interviewing, see especially Cicourel, 1964; Filstead, 1970; the appendices in Whyte, 1955; Lofland, 1966; Lynch, 1977; and Liebow, 1967.)

Individual interviews with 22 members and active participants (the latter hereafter combined with "members") were tape-recorded during the early summer and fall of 1976. Ten ex-members, some of whom had once held important positions in the church, were also individually interviewed. Through discussions and informal interaction with four members who were reluctant to be formally interviewed, I was able to obtain information as to their basic social characteristics—and sometimes a good bit more. Through these informal methods, I also obtained information on six additional ex-members. Data gathered in this fashion were cross-checked during formal interviews with other individuals and through my activities as a participant-observer. There appeared to be few differences in the social characteristics and the basic motives of those who were interviewed formally and those who were not. Nevertheless, I did not include the data obtained through informal interviewing in the collective, percentiled profile of the group.

The interviews with most of the members and two of the younger ex-members were conducted at my office at the institution with which I was affiliated. Members who had been with the church the longest and the remaining ex-members were interviewed in their homes. This was done not only to ensure the cooperation of the ex-members (who did not "know" me and who might have been expected to show less interest in the study), but in order to have access to historical documents and memorabilia—which were readily and copiously volunteered.[1]

The interviews were designed to obtain information as to the social characteristics of the individuals (age, occupation, education, religious background, political orientation, geographical mobility, leisure activities, and so on) and to determine the benefits which the subjects felt they received from participation in the church.

Using the Lofland and Stark (1965) model of conversion as a very general guide, I constructed the following open-ended questions, structured in such a way as to allow maximum flexibility:

(1) When did you discover the Lodge and why were you attracted to it?[2]

(2) Did you experience any tensions or crises in your personal life before or during your initial encounter with the Lodge?[3]

(3) Have any of your close friends been involved in Lodge activities? About how often do you see them in other contexts?

(4) Do your relatives and friends know of your affiliation with the Lodge? If so, how do they feel about it? (Have any of them been involved in psychic or occult activities?)

(5) What do you think you "get" out of participating in Lodge activities? (What keeps you coming back from week to week?)

(6) In what ways are you currently dissatisfied with what you get? (Ex-members were asked why they quit.)

(7) Do you belong to any other organization or groups?[4]

(8) Are there any particular books, ideas, or events which definitely changed your outlook on life?

Most interviews and discussions with members and nonmembers went quite smoothly, due largely to the verbal skills of the interviewees—as will be discussed later, the educational level was relatively high. Many of the subjects were, in fact, quite garrulous, and, although I had imagined the "typical interview" would run a little over one hour, several sessions lasted three or four hours. I found that I was indeed engaged in interaction with literate, middle-class members of the "Occult Establishment."

HISTORY AND ORGANIZATION OF THE CHURCH

At the time I discovered the organization, the Church of the Sun was being characterized to me and to other outsiders as an organization of approximately 30 to 40 members who were devoted to the learning of occult principles and the practice of magic in the "Egyptian Kabbalistic tradition," a fusion of the pagan pantheon of ancient Egypt and the mystical Hebrew "Tree of Life." Indeed, a church-authorized text wove together a fairly systematized cosmology from a variety of occult sources. Much was made of a tripartite model of man drawn from an underground school of occult teachings called "Huna." Seven basic laws of the occult as set forth in a turn-of-the-century publication we might call *The Laws of the Occult Realm* were woven into the church's cosmology, as was a system of color psychology. The latter, in turn, was related to the manifestations of the godhead outlined in the mystical Hebrew Kabbalah and to the deities of ancient Egypt and Greece. There was keen interest in astrology and tarot cards. The cosmology of the Church of the Sun, then, had become something of an occult smorgasbord.

The eclectic nature of the church's teachings was the result of 20 years of "evolutionary drift" of an organization which had originally begun as sort of a mystical, pan-Christian cult. At the center of that cult was a self-trained psychologist and hypnotherapist. The cosmology and rituals of the church in the late 1950s and the early 1960s were not unlike those of the so-called "New Thought" organizations (such as Christian Science and the Church of Religious Science). There were lectures by Harold, group singing from Christian hymnals, and collective prayer and meditation, the latter hypnotically induced and guided by Harold. Christmas was celebrated, and there were church bazaars. As the 1960s progressed, however, membership grew to approximately 75 to 80 members. The little cult became a small church with "branch fellowships" in nearby areas (or it might be better termed as "established cult"—see Ellwood, 1973: 22). A select group of "Apostles" was formed (mostly from the ranks of the early members), and an even more elite group, the "Elders," was later drawn from the Apostles. The church was reorganized about an hierarchical system of "color lodges" in the late 1960s. In this new order, one's degree of spiritual advancement was reflected in his or her color lodge membership (red for newer members, yellow for the somewhat more advanced, orange for the still more advanced, and so on). However, before this system could be fully realized, another reorganization took place in 1973—the First Order of the Inner Circle of Isis was formed. The Elders were still recognized as the traditional elite, and a Board of

Directors still took care of business matters. But it became clear to most that the "people who mattered" were members of the First Order—which did not include all the Elders and Apostles, and which did include some rather new members. (A Second Order was started the following year, and it was clearly regarded as just that—"second" in all respects.)

The changing organizational structure of the Church of the Sun reflected the waxing influence of paganism, ritual magic, and other "hard-core" occult concepts—such as the search for "alternative realities" à la Carlos Castaneda (1968, 1971, 1973, 1974). The drift into paganism and ritual magic alienated many of the middle-aged and older people, most of whom had been members for several years. They felt that the magical rituals were becoming ends in themselves, and that the quest for unity with "God-the-Father," the chief goal emphasized in the early pan-Christian teachings, was being ignored. And, as in Marty's characterization of the "Occult Establishment," these people were offended by the tales concerning the use of alcohol and (possibly) drugs for purposes of achieving transcendence by "opening doors into alternative realities" in the rites of the Inner Circle of Isis.

Several of the more traditional and conservative members and ex-members began meeting informally on a once-a-month basis to discuss various "metaphysical" issues (the terms "magic" and "occult" were almost never employed). Meanwhile, the more "radical" group of younger, "hard-core" occultists also began meeting informally. In short, the cult-turned-church was now faced with the formation of dissident sects.

SOCIAL CHARACTERISTICS
OF MEMBERS AND EX-MEMBERS

In spite of doctrinal differences, however, the 22 members and the 10 ex-members who were formally interviewed were basically similar—they tended to be middle-aged, middle-class, and middle-of-the-road in terms of political views and life styles. With the exception of one chicano, all were white. The median age for members was 37; a few ex-members were quite young (in their twenties); most were somewhat older (in their early fifties or sixties).

Of the 32 persons formally interviewed, 23 were females. Thirty-five percent of them were housepersons (some with part-time sales jobs), 30% were employed in low-level white collar work, and 22% were teachers. Three of the nine males were self-employed (one was an artist and two were businessmen with incomes in excess of $25,000), one was a college professor, three were in low-level white collar jobs, one was a maintenance man, and another was a graduate student. The median family annual income for all those formally interviewed was $15,000; the figure for individuals was $12,500. Slightly more than 80% of all those interviewed had annual incomes in excess of $10,000.

Virtually all of those interviewed were high school graduates. Twenty-three percent of the members had obtained (or were close to obtaining) a Master's degree. One member had a doctorate, as did one of the ex-members.[5]

In terms of religious background the 47% who were once Protestant and nearly 16% who were once Catholic tended to be religious drop-outs. They had stopped attending these respective "mainline" churches in their teens. However, another 25% of those formally interviewed had moved into the Church of the Sun from either recent or life-long participation in either Christian Science or the Church of Religious Science. The factors which led all of these middle-class, relatively conventional people to become involved in the occult are discussed below.

CONVERSION AND COMMITMENT TO THE OCCULT

Figure 1 portrays the conversion and commitment processes in the Church of the Sun. Is the model applicable only to that one group, or only to the occult subculture? The answer is probably both yes and no. Yes, insofar as some aspects of the framework are particularly salient in the occult conversion process—Phase I, for example. No, in that many aspects of the process will be

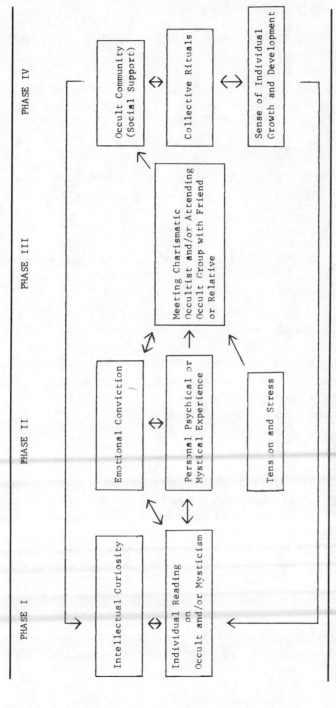

Figure 1: Descriptive Model of Conversion and Commitment to the Occult

recognized as easily generalized and compatible with conversion and commitment to a variety of perspectives in a variety of settings—see Festinger et al. (1956), Catton (1957), Simmons (1964), and Lofland and Stark (1965). Therefore, the sequential pattern in Figure 1 should be viewed as empirically grounded, yet transsituational in some respects. It is also a broadly descriptive framework rather than a more determinant causal one. The arrows represent merely the probable direction of influence of one sequence or part of a sequence upon other elements in the framework.

PHASE I: "I read this book. . ."

As previously mentioned, conventional religious perspectives tended not to satisfy questions about the nature of the self and the universe posed by the people who became involved in the Church of the Sun. It is difficult to estimate what percentage of the general population allows such questions and curiosity to draw them into serious reading on occult topics. However, nearly two-thirds of the persons formally interviewed had let such curiosity beckon them toward reading a book on such matters, in the vast majority of cases before (often *long* before) they encountered the Church of the Sun. Retrospectively, they regarded the reading of such a book or books as an important "turning point" in their lives. The range of authors and topics mentioned by the interviewees covered the full panoply of the occult and mysticism, ranging from books by Montgomery on reincarnation, Crowley on the practice of "magick," Fortune on "psychic self defense" and "the goddess," any number of books about Cayce, astrology texts, and books by Eastern and/or Western mystics. Some of the subjects' lives were immediately altered by such experiences. For others, however, the phenomena about which they had read did not take on immediate significance. Whatever the case, more active involvement in the occult subculture awaited the development of (1) a first-hand, personal psychical or mystical experience, and/or (2) encountering a group of people with similar interests. In other words, as a result of their own curiosity and reading about the occult, most of the subjects were *latent* occultists and not *active* seekers.

People continually raise meaningful questions about matters which dominant societal institutions (particularly science and religion) have defined as hogwash or heresy, simply because such matters lie beyond the officially defined "natural order of things." Individuals alone and in groups can independently and critically reflect upon and transcend their own perspectives and environment in a therapeutic fashion. Human beings are innately—if only sporadically—curious, intelligent, meaning-seeking agents, who read and reflect upon books. None of these statements should surprise social scientists. Yet the models of conversion which have generally been employed in studying new religious and occult groups (if any frameworks are used at all)[6] tend to tactitly deny their subjects such dignified characteristics. (For a more general and useful counterstatement to such tendencies, see Morris, 1976.) From the deterministic, behavioristic theories of "brainwashing" to the somewhat more flexible framework of Lofland and Stark (1965), there exist background assumptions to the effect that men are *not* active, critical, self-reflexive creatures. Rather, men are held to be passive agents of social forces, headless beings manipulated by environmental and situational factors. In addition, there is also the frequent implication that *weltanschauungen* which lie outside the world-views authorized by science and/or mainstream religious institutions are somehow "deviant" and lacking in validity.

Most of the persons observed and interviewed in the Church of the Sun and in other occult groups have not struck me as particularly passive or deviant. It is true that these individuals seek knowledge about themselves and the universe through mystical transcendence. And to accomplish this aim, they employ magical and occult beliefs and techniques, collective ritual, and hypnosis. However, these are probably best seen as merely technical alternatives to involvement in psychiatry, conventional religious study and worship, political activities, and "crusades," not to mention the "therapies" of alcohol and/or drugs. With the partial exception of the latter, the more "conventional" techniques of identity-building, learning, and coping just listed were found to be unsatisfying and unfulfilling to the occultists who had tried them. For the vast majority of the subjects, occult principles and techniques "worked."

Thus, people attracted to the occult perspective of the Church of the Sun, as well as to many other "countercultural religious perspectives," have been, for the most part, rather "average," middle-class, thinking human beings—though perhaps better educated and more tolerant (see Wuthnow, 1976). And, like many an "average citizen" of the mid- to late-1960s, the persons drawn into the Church of the Sun occasionally browsed through books on the occult and once in a while stopped to read. What factors led them to become more deeply involved in the occult, while their fellow "average citizens" remained outside? This question brings us to Phases II and III.

PHASE II: "When it happens to you. . ."

It is likely that a significant number of those who become involved in the occult subculture do so not only because they have read a book or two on such matters and have become intellectually stimulated—something more is needed. That additional factor is often a first-hand experience of the "nonordinary realities" of the occult realm. Forty percent of the members and 30% of the ex-members of the Church of the Sun described a personal psychical or mystical experience which occurred prior to their encountering the church as a "major turning point" in their lives. Many others also mentioned such episodes as having occurred prior to their encounter with the church—but they did not define them as a major turning point. (For a few subjects this was due to the fact that they had been experiencing psychical or paranormal events since childhood; they claimed to be "psychically gifted" to some extent.) The most frequently mentioned types of experience were those of precognition (in dreams or during the waking hours), astral projection, déjà vu, and telepathy.[7]

These episodes served to verify on a personal level phenomena about which they had merely read or heard. Those who had been skeptical were shaken. The subjects dismissed the suggestion that such an experience might have been the product of suggestion. To the contrary, they emphatically maintained that "what happened to me was *real*" and was not the result of suggestion or idle fantasy. Indeed, some were temporarily puzzled by the vividness or "reality" of their sampling of the supernatural; they did not necessarily seek or like what they had seen or felt. Furthermore, in some cases, Phases I and II and reversed: the psychical event preceded any reading on the occult.[8] Whatever the sequence, though, in Phase II, rational, book-bred curiosity became fused with emotional conviction and a desire to know more. Frequently, however, the desire could be fulfilled only upon the discovery of the Church and its leader.

A second factor in Phase II which led many in the direction of the Church of the Sun is a common one to the conversion process: tension and stress. Approximately 44% of all those formally interviewed reported high levels of tension and stress, and an additional 22% reported more moderate levels. Most of these tensions and anxieties were the result of marital problems or of identity crises resulting from problems with occupational, age, or sex roles. Some were vaguely experiencing a "meaning crisis," that is, an anxiety arising from feelings that there "must be something more to life" than the ordinary secular routines. However, it should also be pointed out that a full 41% of the subjects in the study reported no problems or tensions at the time of conversion. In fact, a number of these people went out of their way to point out that things had "never been better."

Tension and stress, as the model in Figure 1 indicates, appears to have been totally unrelated to prior acquaintance with occult literature. Insofar as tension and stress are sometimes thought to be associated with paranormal experiences, there were some persons under high or moderate stress who, at about the same time, underwent a paranormal episode. However, there were just as many, if not more, who did not. Therefore, I think tension and stress is an independent factor related to either the reading of occult literature or physical or mystical experiences. It was a variable, however, in predisposing some 60% of the members toward the cosmology, techniques, and the leadership style of the Church of the Sun. Note, however, that this study does not include a traditional control group for comparison purposes, a possible point of criticism (see Heirich, 1977, for a discussion of this issue and some evidence *against* tension-oriented theories of conversion).

PHASE III: "It was all so new and exciting. . ."

The third phase of the model is the most easily generalized. Jargon aside, Phase III might be more precisely and succinctly summed up as either "meeting my guru" or "meeting the right people at the right time and in the right place." Based on information obtained in the interviews (both formal and informal), both the church and its leader initially impressed these middle-class, respectable, congenial people as middle-class, respectable, and congenial. Topics of long-standing (though sometimes dormant) interest could be pursued in a comfortable setting. People were polite and open, not doctrinaire and pushy. There was humor and warmth rather than sober intensity and fanatical camaraderie. And, furthermore, the setting stayed that way.

Another half of the people formally and informally interviewed reported a degree of fascination with the leader, mostly because of the knowledge he possessed. In style and manner, too, the leader was the perfect low-key charismatic leader for this sector of the growing "Occult Establishment." A self-educated psychologist and hypnotherapist, he presented a scholarly, fatherly, erudite appearance without being at all overbearing. He had a keen sense of humor, his face was open and understanding, his voice was authoritative.

The formats of study and worship were also respectably middle-class for the most part. During the week there were classes on astrology, palmistry, aura-reading, the tarot, and other occult topics. A Sunday morning (later changed to Saturday evening) worship service held weekly began and ended with inoffensive pagan invocations and benedictions. A scholarly lecture was sometimes the central feature of these services. As the early 1970s progressed, however, there were more and more full-blown pagan rituals which went on at some length. A great deal of "ritual work" went on in the First Order of the Inner Circle of Isis.

People were usually introduced to the church by attending a class or a devotional service with a friend or relative, typically a spouse. Others found out about the church through an occult supply shop owned, in part, by the leader. In the early days, according to some, members were frequently drawn from his professional clientele when he was still a practicing psychologist. Apparently this process was on the wane, however, for only about 10% of the persons interviewed stated that they had discovered the church in this manner.

PHASE IV: "The church is our home. . ."

Once people become involved in an occult group, what keeps them there? Here, again, we find a factor common to conversion and commitment to other types of perspectives—emotional bonds. Fully 47% of all those formally interviewed stated that the group was "like a family" or "like home" to them. An additional 22% were somewhat more restrained, stating that one of the major reasons for their continued involvement was that they "liked the people." Yet the Church of the Sun was far from being a total or communal institution. Why, then, the intensity of good feeling? For one thing, the members did little else. Sixty percent quickly admitted that they belonged to no other social, political, or cultural groups whatsoever, while membership in any such organizations (generally P.T.A. or a professional association) for the remaining 44% tended to be nominal at best. Very few people had social lives unrelated to church activities. Even most of the ex-members' social activities centered around monthly meetings of ex-members and older, alienated members.

Some people remained involved solely for these social reasons. Most, however, had other goals. Balch and Taylor's (1976) observation that growth and spiritual development are general aims of most people involved in the occult subculture was confirmed by the finding that nearly 60% of those formally interviewed in my research gave "inward or spiritual development" as a reason for participating in the Church of the Sun. In a related finding, nearly 44% mentioned that they had obtained a new or more positive self-image in more secular terms. While some respondents indicated that this was a by-product of their more metaphysical or inner growth, others saw their new and more positive identities in entirely secular or psychological terms.

Twenty-eight percent explicitly emphasized that they remained in the church because of the continuous sense of mystery, curiosity, and excitement they felt in church activities. Such feelings were implicit in the comments of a good many others. In addition, most members, particularly the younger ones, warmed to the feelings of challenge and hardship which were supposedly involved in progressively mastering occult principles and techniques. The group was warned repeatedly of the discipline and diligence required to unlock the mysteries of both their inner selves and the universe. These warnings did much to add to a sense of meaning and purposiveness to Church activities. (This favorable response to discipline and hardship is similar to that in the Hare Krishna movement described by Stone, 1976).

To sum, then, what we have found is confirmation of the often ignored sociological truism that people obtain and deepen their individual identities best within functional, cohesive groups (see Nisbet, 1953).[9] Yet I think it is necessary to probe more deeply this dialectical relationship between community cohesiveness and individual identity. Collins (1975) has suggested that human cognition, especially language and religion, is built upon animal-based emotional bonds through social rituals. He arrived at this insight through his reinterpretation of the work of Durkheim:

> Durkheim's insight into the social nature of cognition is similar to that of Mead and also that of Freud . . . Durkheim's model of ritual behavior gives the most fruitful means for understanding how it operates; for language, the basis of human civilization, is fundamentally ritualistic in the sense just described. It requires a group of at least two persons. It focuses their attention by formalizing the gesture (in this case, the sound) so that its arbitrarily

repetitive qualities are the essence of the experience. It calls forth a common emotional (we may say more generally, a perceptual-experimental) response, which it serves to select out and reinforce by mutual attention, and it provides a symbol (an idea) transcending the here and now of concrete experience and making it recallable in other contents. Human language, in other words is the evocation of animal social bonds strengthened and focused by stereotyping and attached to the human capacity for symbolization [Collins, 1975: 96]

Collins (1975: 97) also takes care to point out that "it is the non-verbal signals in which verbal formulas are embedded that holds human rituals together."

Collins work gives us a much-needed new look at the importance and place of social rituals in our lives in general and in the religious sphere in particular. His studies reemphasize the power of collective symbolic rituals to effect at the deepest levels individual emotions and cognitions. With specific regard to the occult organization I have called the Church of the Sun, it seemed that collective rituals were highly effective in promoting cohesion and in the formation of the individual self-concepts. Symbolic social ritual was at the heart of the dynamics of the Church.

That collective ritual was employed with such effectiveness in the Church of the Sun was, undoubtedly, due to the training and skills of its leader. He had been, after all, a practicing psychologist with a great deal of knowledge of the work Jung and skilled in the use of hypnotic techniques. In addition, the person who had come to be recognized as second-in-command also had considerable experience and skills in the magical arts. To be sure, the format of the rituals gradually changed over the 20-year history of the organization, moving from pan-Christian ceremonies to pagan-inspired magical rituals. Many of the older, more traditional members weathered the transition to the more "hard-core" occult perspective and techniques, and some gave testimony to the power of the new ways. Even those who did not survive the transition and quit the Church attested to the powers of the rituals. They liked and claimed considerable benefit from the older pan-Christian mystic rituals. But the new ones bothered them so deeply and the emotional and cognitive dissonance generated was so great that they left the Church.[10] So powerful was the impact of the rituals that many left in spite of the fact that all, or nearly all, of their friends were fellow church members. "I tried to adjust, but I just couldn't do it," said one subject who seemed close to tears.

Newer members were generally fulfilled in the new rituals, except when they were not properly performed. Unfortunately, this occurred more often than many would have liked, because the leader, though a good enough socioemotional leader, was inept at many organizational tasks. In the rituals I observed, several people did appear to be quite emotionally involved, later testifying that they did indeed sense "another reality" or that "doors had opened." I did not directly experience the more intense rituals which were reported to have transpired in the First Circle of the Inner Circle of Isis.

The processes in Phase IV tended to feed back into other aspects of the model, producing increased reading in the occult and more frequent sensations of the supernatural order. This, in turn, fostered community solidarity, self-knowledge which led to more reading and psychic experiences, and so on.

CONCLUSION

Based on observations of and interviews with members and ex-members of an occult organization which I have called the Church of the Sun, the route of conversion and commitment to an occult perspective appears to be a complex one, a process which generally takes several years. Typically, it begins either with individual reading on occult topics or with a personal psychical or mystical event; one experience then leads to the other. More active involvement in the occult, however, usually awaits the "proper" time and setting, and people, a situation often discovered by accident and generally through informal means. Characteristics of the setting and the group tend to be congruent with those of the individuals (see also Scott, 1976).

Upon discovering and liking the setting and the people in it, the individual is then exposed to collective symbolic rituals which act to increase the solidarity of the group and to structure and/or restructure individual cognitive processes. Involvement in an occult group of community, in turn, fosters more reading on occult topics and increases the frequency of psychical or mystical personal experiences.

It is important to point out that these social psychological processes operate within a specific sociohistorical setting. Conversion and commitment to the occult is easier and more likely today than it was 15 or 20 years ago. This is due in part to the "occult explosion" of the past decade or so from which an "Occult Establishment" has emerged. These events, in turn, have been the product of the turbulence and relentless questioning of the 1960s and early 1970s, a time in which the very foundations of the Western, rationalistic, and scientific views of man and the universe have been severely shaken (see Lynch, 1975). The reading and discussion of occult literature and the sharing of personal psychical experiences is much more likely to be tolerated today than ever before—more so in certain geographical and social settings than in others, to be sure. Yet the "Occult Establishment" is a growing and widespread social phenomenon which can no longer be dismissed as a "fad." It is high time we devoted more study to how and why people are drawn into the occult subculture, and to how they may be harmed or benefited by such experiences.

NOTES

1. While Douglas' book on *Investigative Social Research* (1976) had not yet appeared, I followed many of his strategies. It was quite easy to build friendly and cooperative relations with most members of the church. The degree of cooperation and candor did indeed seem remarkable. As Douglas has suggested, I tried to absorb as much as possible about the life and the world-view of the members through direct experience of their activities. However, I also subscribe, at least in part, to Douglas' conflict perspective. Therefore, particularly when it came to historical and organizational matters to which I did not have direct access, I attempted to "check-out" and validate information, as well as to penetrate various fronts, evasions, and deceptions—few though there seem to have been.

Checking-out key portions of information was not difficult to do; as soon as possible I engaged in formal and informal "elite interviewing" (see Dexter, 1970) of members who were in various key or strategic positions. Information obtained in these initial and lengthy discussions were then used in constructing the format for the interviews with the rank-and-file. Thus, in interviews with the later, in as natural a fashion as possible, I would insert such questions as "Is that about the time Harold's divorce occurred?" or "Didn't you and James join the Lodge at about the same time?" or "What did you think of the use of intoxicating agents in some of the meetings of the Inner Circle of Isis? Did you ever suspect the use of drugs in this?" I generally tried to begin asking such questions early in the interview process, thus serving to inform the subjects that I had a certain amount of familiarity with the Lodge and even knew of some embarrassing or controversial episodes in the organization.

2. The term "Lodge" was used rather than "Church" because, at the time of the study, the organization was increasingly being referred to by the leader and the members as a secret, occult "mystery school" or "white lodge."

3. When a few subjects looked puzzled or asked for further clarification, I suggested examples of problems or tensions with marital partners or other family members or friends, problems at work or school, or any particular "hang-ups" or "identity crises."

4. In order to insure that the subjects did not mistake "other groups" to mean other religious or occult groups, I probed for membership in social, political, professional, or cultural groups or associations.

5. The doctorates were in the social sciences. I am not including myself in this tabulation or in any other.

6. While many of the more recent studies on new religious groups (such as those in Glock and Bellah, 1976) and on the occult (such as Scott, 1976) are rich in descriptive detail, they tend to be rather atheoretical.

7. The incidence of the psychical or mystical events amongst the general population may be greater than has been supposed (see Greeley, 1975).

8. Almost all of the subjects who underwent a psychical experience before doing any reading on the occult were relatively young (20s to mid-30s). To a great extent, this may represent a "generational phenomenon "in that many of them came of age in the more psychically conscious period of the 1960s.

9. It has also long been held in the sociology of religion that one of religion's primary functions is to deepen and spiritualize the identity of the individual adherents (see O'Dea, 1966).

10. Virtually all of the older ex-members indicated that the shift to the paganistic "hard-core" occult and magical practices and philosophy was a major reason (generally *the* major reason) for their leaving.

REFERENCES

BALCH, R. W. and D. TAYLOR (1976) "Walking out the door of the rest of your life: becoming a member of a contemporary UFO cult." Paper presented at the meetings of the Pacific Sociological Association, March 26.
CASTANEDA, C. (1974) Tales of Power. New York: Simon & Schuster.

———— (1973) Journey to Ixtlan. New York: Simon & Schuster.

———— (1971) A Separate Reality: Further Conversations with Don Jaun. New York: Simon & Schuster.

———— (1968) The Teachings of Don Juan: A Yaqui Way of Knowledge. Berkeley: Univ. of California Press.

CATTON, W. R. (1957) "What kind of people does a religious cult attract?" Amer. Soc. Rev. 22 (October): 561-566.

CICOUREL, A. (1964) Method and Measurement in Sociology. New York: Free Press.

DEXTER, L. A. (1970) Elite and Specialized Interviewing. Evanston, Ill: Northwestern Univ. Press.

DOUGLAS, J. D. (1976) Investigative Social Research: Individual and Team Field Research. Beverly Hills, CA: Sage.

ELIADE, M. (1976) Occultism, Witchcraft, and Cultural Fashions. Chicago: Univ. of Chicago Press.

ELLWOOD, R. S. (1973) Religious and Spiritual Groups in Modern America. Englewood Cliffs, N.J.: Prentice-Hall.

FESTINGER, L., H. W. RIEKEN and S. SCHACHTER (1956) When Prophecy Fails. Minneapolis: Univ. of Minnesota Press.

FILSTEAD, W. [ed.] (1970) Qualitative Methodology: Firsthand Involvement with the Social World. Chicago: Markham.

FREEDLAND, N. (1972) The Occult Explosion. New York: Berkley Medalian Books.

GLOCK, C. Y. and R. N. BELLAH [eds.] (1976) The New Religious Consciousness. Berkeley and Los Angeles: Univ. of California Press.

GODWIN, J. (1972) Occult America. Garden City, NY: Doubleday.

GREELEY, A. (1975) The Sociology of the Paranormal: A Reconnaissance. Beverly Hills, CA: Sage.

———— (1970) "Implications for the sociology of religion of occult behavior in the youth culture." Paper presented at the 1970 meetings of the American Sociological Association.

GREENFIELD, R. (1975) The Spiritual Supermarket: An Account of Gurus Gone Public in America. New York: Saturday Review Press.

HIERICH, M. (1977) "Change of heart: a test of some widely held theories about religious conversion." Forthcoming, Amer. J. of Sociology.

HOLZER, H. (1974) The Dictionary of the Occult. New York: Henry Regnery.

————(1973) The Witchcraft Report. New York: Ace.

———— (1972) The New Pagans. Garden City, NY: Doubleday.

JOHNSON, G. (1976) "The Hare Krishna in San Francisco," pp. 31-52 in C. Y. Glock and R. N. Bellah (eds.) The New Religious Consciousness. Berkeley: Univ. of California Press.

LIEBOW, E. (1967) Tally's Corner. Boston: Little, Brown.

LOFLAND, J. (1966) Doomsday Cult. Englewood Cliffs, NJ: Prentice-Hall.

———— and R. STARK (1965) "Becoming a world-saver: a theory of conversion to a deviant perspective." Amer. Soc. Rev. 30 (December): 862-875.

LYNCH, FREDERICK R. (1977) "Field research and future history: problems posed for ethnographers by the 'Doomsday Cult' making good." Forthcoming, Amer. Sociologist.

———— (1975) "Sociology and parapsychology." J. of Parapsychology 39 (December): 97-105.

MARTY, M. (1970) "The occult establishment." Social Research 37 (Summer): 212-230.

MATHISON, R. R. (1960) Faiths, Cults, and Sects in America: From Atheism to Zen. Indianapolis and New York: Bobbs-Merrill.

MORRIS, M. B. (1976) An Excursion into Creative Sociology. New York: Columbia Univ. Press.

NISBET, R. A. (1953) Quest for Community. New York: Oxford Univ. Press.

O'DEA, T. F. (1966) The Sociology of Religion. Englewood Cliffs, NJ: Prentice-Hall.

SCOTT, G. (1976) "Social structure and the occult: a sociological analysis of the social organization, behavior patterns and beliefs of two occult groups: a spiritual growth group and a witchcraft group." Unpublished Ph.D. dissertation, University of California, Berkeley.

SIMMONS, J. L. (1964) "On maintaining deviant belief systems: a case study." Social Problems 11 (Winter): 250-257.

STONE, D. (1976) "The human potential movement," pp. 93-116 in C. Y. Glock and R. N. Bellah (eds.) The New Religious Consciousness. Berkeley: Univ. of California Press.

TIRYAKIAN, E. A. [ed.] (1974) On the Margin of the Visible: Sociology, the Esoteric and the Occult. New York: John Wiley.

——— (1973) "Toward the sociology of esoteric culture." Amer. J. of Sociology 78 (November): 491-512.

TRUZZI, M. (1974a) "Definitions and dimensions of the occult: towards a sociological perspective," pp. 243-257 in E. A. Tiryakian (ed.) On the Margin of the Visible: Sociology, the Esoteric and the Occult. New York: John Wiley.

——— (1974b) "Towards a sociology of the occult: notes on modern witchcraft," pp. 628-645 in I. I. Zaretsky and M. P. Leone (eds.) Religious Movements in Contemporary America. Princeton, NJ: Princeton Univ. Press.

——— (1972) "The occult revival as popular culture: some random observations on the old and nouveau witch." Soc. Q. 13 (Winter): 16-36.

WALLIS, R. (1974) "The Aetherius society: a case study in the formation of a mystagogic congregation." Soc. Rev. 22 (February): 27-45.

WEBB, J. (1974) The Occult Underground. LaSalle, IL: Open Court Publishing.

WHYTE, W. F. (1955) Street Corner Society. Chicago: Univ. of Chicago Press.

WILSON, C. (1973) The Occult. New York: Vintage.

WOLFE, T. (1976) "The me decade and the third great awakening." New West 1 (August 30): 27-50.

WUTHNOW, R. (1976) "The new religions in social context, pp. 267-295 in C. Y. Glock and R. N. Bellah (eds.) The New Religious Consciousness. Berkeley: Univ. of California Press.

ZARETSKY, I. I. and M. P. LEONE [eds.] (1974) Religious Movements in Contemporary America. Princeton, NJ: Princeton Univ. Press.

*Simmonds has gathered the only personality assessment data known about for partici-
pants in the Jesus movement and uses some of it here to support his provocative idea that
conversion to the movement does not entail conversion in the traditional sense of the term,
but instead represents a shift in addiction.*

Conversion or Addiction

Consequences of Joining
a Jesus Movement Group

ROBERT B. SIMMONDS
State University of New York, Cortland

The rise and flowering of the Jesus movement during the late
1960s and early 1970s raised questions regarding the reasons why
many people who had previously engaged in drug-oriented life-
styles would undergo conversion to a fundamentalist Christian
belief system. In order to address these questions, it is important
to look at the kind of people who joined this movement, and to
explore the nature of their conversion experiences and how such
might be related to subsequent commitment within a Jesus
movement group.

The basic arguments which will be put forth are that (1) the
personality profiles of members of a Jesus movement group on
which this research was done are consistent with previous research which has shown that religious people in general are

Author's Note: *This research was supported in part by a University of
Nevada Research Advisory Board grant, for which appreciation is
expressed.*

ROBERT B. SIMMONDS is a faculty member in the Department of Sociology of the
State University of New York at Cortland. He completed his doctorate in Social Psychology at the University of Nevada, Reno, doing his work on the same Jesus movement
group described in his paper for his issue.

[113]

described in terms of greater dependency than are the religious; (2) the conversion experience in the Jesus Movement may serve to resolve personal problems which had been experienced prior to conversion, but without changing basic personality patterns; and (3) there is very little evidence of subsequent personality change after a member has been the group for a while. The implication of these arguments is that these people have basically stable personality patterns, both prior to and after affiliation with a religious group. This pattern, however, is characterized in terms of dependency on an external source of gratification, such that a description in terms of the "addictive" personality might be useful. The data used in this paper were originally gathered for another purpose (see Simmonds, 1977), but this post hoc analysis of these data seems suggestive and useful.

PREVIOUS RESEARCH

There is some evidence to indicate that religious people in general tend to exhibit dependency on some external source of gratification. Black and London (1966) found a high positive correlation between the variables of obedience to parents and country and indices of religious belief such as church attendance, belief in God, and prayer. Goldsen, et al. (1960) showed that people who were more religious consistently showed tendencies toward greater social conformity than did the nonreligious, a finding consistent with the notion that religious people seek external approval. These results are supported by Fisher (1964), who reported that a measure of social approval and religion were strongly associated. Religious people show dependence not only on social values, but also on other external agents. Duke (1964) found that church attendance indicated more responsiveness to the effects of a placebo. In a study of 50 alcoholics, it was found that those who were dependent on alcohol were more likely to have had a religious background (Walters, 1957). (See Simmonds et al., 1976, for a more thorough discussion of the ideas of this paragraph.)

A number of theories suggest than conversion to a fundamentalist religious perspective serves to resolve preexisting
personal conflicts within members. Once these conflicts are
resolved by religious affiliation, there is no reason to expect that
personality changes would occur over time in the group. Any
personality changes occurring in the process would happen at the
point of conversion, since former conflicts would no longer be
present, and self-definitions after conversion would reflect the
absence of these conflicts. This argument is consistent with some
anecdotal evidence offered by members of the Jesus movement
group examined in this paper. Some members said that the
moment of conversion was the most beautiful of their lives, that
they felt that all of their previous conflicts had been resolved,
and that they were at the point committed to a steadfast experience in "serving the Lord." They emphasized that their rebirth
in Jesus implied that they were then to follow "the straight and
narrow path" and never to "divert their eyes," that they wanted
to continue to experience the beauty of the movement of conversion. In conformity with the definition of the group suggested by
residents, the group experience represented a place where former
sinners could come to serve the Lord. Once a person had been
"saved," s/he was "living with the Lord," and there was no subsequent need to be concerned about conflicts.

Adams and Fox (1972), in a study of another Jesus movement
group, suggested that part of the motivation for a person to join
the movement is to resolve a role-identity crisis, even if affiliation
represented a pseudosolution to the crisis. These authors point
out that adolescents face a personal crisis at the onset of puberty
with reference to accepting sexual feelings, learning to live with
them, and then facing the responsibility of adult role behavior.
Instead of growing normally, facing the turmoil which usually
accompanies these changes, and incorporating new identities,
Adams and Fox concluded that members of the Jesus movement
cling to childhood morality, with its black-and-white, all-or-
nothing judgments. Fundamentalist Christian doctrine provides
an ideology based on personal, internal, and unexplainable
experiences, rather than on rational, critical analysis. It provides
a comprehensive world view and, as such, buffers the convert
against normal growth experiences which are grounded in

reality. Because these young Christians found themselves in this secure environment, the conflicts which they had been facing previously were postponed, and they had no further motivation to change.

Another theory which leads to the inference that affiliation helps to resolve previous conflicts is Glock's (1964) extension of deprivation theory. He suggests that people will attempt to compensate for felt deprivation with either secular or religious resolutions. People who feel various forms of deprivation will be motivated to achieve a secular resolution when they feel that they have the power in the real world to eliminate the causes of the deprivation. Religious resolutions, on the other hand, tend, Glock says, to compensate for feelings of deprivation rather than to eliminate them. It might be suggested, then, that religious affiliation would serve to resolve previous conflicts, and that, since these conflicts would no longer exist, there would be no reason to suggest that personality responses would change across time in a religious group.

An analysis consistent with this notion is presented by Gordon (1974). He suggests that the Jesus movement combines elements of the moral code into which converts were originally socialized. Conversion, then, can be said to represent an identity synthesis which "consolidates" two different universes of discourse. Religion establishes and legitimates a unified identity for the convert. When this consolidation is made, the believer experiences a release from guilt and upset. Gordon states that people who experience a radical discontinuity between the two universes of discourse, such as those who adopt a radically different religious ideology from the one in which they were originally socialized, are likely to experience emotional upset. The Jesus people, however, consolidate identities from childhood Christian experiences and the hip drug subculture, creating a smooth, guilt-free synthesis. The convert's identity problems are resolved in the Jesus movement by coming into contact with people who share the same beliefs, by participating in activities which identify them with others of their own generation, and by having close contact with those who have also been in the drug subculture. Gordon observes that religion serves as an arbitrator between contradictory social roles because it transcends these roles and organizes them on the basis of higher meaning. This fusion of identities resolves many conflicts which these converts had been experiencing previously. Life within the group becomes a comparatively easy existence. Few or no emotional problems regarding identity or self-definition would occur after affiliation with the group.

These theories all suggest that conversion represents a solution to personal conflicts which these people had been experiencing previously, and they further imply that once a person converts there is no necessary reason for her/him to experience resocialization toward a psychologically "healthier" pattern. On the other hand, Robbins (1969), in studying a Meher Baba group, the residents of which displayed many of the same behavioral patterns prior to conversion as those seen in members of the Jesus movement, suggests that conversion and subsequent affiliation experiences need not lead to subsequent static personality patterns. Because of the nature of this Meher Baba group, residents were encouraged to strengthen their ties with more conventional life pursuits, such as getting a job, cutting their hair, and so on. By implication, members of the Meher Baba group would be expected to develop personality patterns after affiliation which would probably become more like those of the normative population than those of new affiliates.

The same implication is seen in a study by Mauss and Petersen (1974), who postulated that the main function of the Jesus movement for converts may be one of providing a "waystation to respectability" for those youths who were in the process of reabsorption into the dominant society. The usual route to this "return to respectability" for members of the group they studied was through membership in more established Pentecostal churches.

The data analyzed in the present report appear to be somewhat in contradiction to the conclusions reported by Robbins and by Mauss and Petersen. Specifically, personality data were gathered on residents of a Jesus movement group at two points over a two and one-half month interval, and, as will be described subsequently, there was no evidence of personality change across this time period in the group. Methodological considerations, however, may have accounted for this lack of change, although not necessarily. It is possible that the two and one-half month period between testings was not long enough for any evidence of personality self-description changes to become apparent. Furthermore, the nature of the personality tests or the context in which the personality tests were administered may have led to a false conclusion that there was no change across time in the group. Thus, the findings of Robbins and of Mauss and Petersen on other groups are not necessarily contradicted by the post hoc analysis presented in this report.

DESCRIPTION OF THE GROUP

The fundamentalist Jesus movement group studied here is part of a larger organization which is based primarily on the West Coast, but which has a large number of branch houses located throughout the nation (and a few outside the United States). Because of an agreement made with leaders of this organization, the identity of the group cannot be revealed in published literature (this group is *not* the Children of God). About 100 residents were living at a farm owned by the organization in 1972 when a survey was conducted on 96 members (69 males and 27 females) by an interview team of seven researchers.

The mean age of the members was 20.8 years, with an age range of 16 to 34 years. The residents had completed an average of 12.04 years of formal education, although only 66 (69%) had completed high school. Nineteen of the 69 males had served in the armed forces. Only 53 (55%) had come from homes in which their parents were still married. Most of those interviewed had come from relatively large families (with an average of 3.97 children per family). Their parents were relatively affluent, with 52 of the respondents reporting a mean annual parental income of $16,250 (a sizable minority claimed not to know family income). Fathers of the respondents had completed a mean of 12.47 years of formal education, and mothers had completed 11.93 years. Twenty-three of the residents had participated in political activity prior to conversion. A large porportion (81) had attended church during childhood, with 51% of them coming from Protestant backgrounds, 27% from Catholic, 2% from Jewish, and 8% from other religious backgrounds (e.g., Mormon and Greek Orthodox).

Residents of the commune believed in a strict and literal interpretation of the Bible. They believed in hard work "for the Lord" and a total dedication to their personal "walk with Jesus." Although there has been continual change in their policies with reference to sex roles (cf. Harder et al., 1976), they still believed in the relative superiority of men over women. Pastors of the group held nearly absolute authority over other members (the "brothers" and "sisters"). Life within the commune was very regimented, but it also provided a meaningful belief system, food and shelter, and close interpersonal relations for members. More elaborate descriptions of various segments of the organization can be found in Harder et al. (1972), Harder (1974), Simmonds et al. (1974), Harder et al. (1976), Richardson et al. (1975, 1977), Simmonds et al. (1976), Simmonds (1976a, 1976b).

METHOD

Gough's (1952) Adjective Check List (ACL) and Spielberger's (1968) State-Trait Anxiety Inventory (STAI) were administered to 96 members (69 males and 27 females) of the group described above. These tests were administered in individual sessions in conjunction with a lengthy face-to-face interview with each member. The ACL is composed of 300 descriptive adjectives which reflect personality patterns based on 24 different variables. The STAI reflects, through level of agreement with certain statements, the degree to which respondents experience anxiety as a general pattern in their lives, as well as the degree to which respondents experience anxiety at the time of the testing. These results were then compared with scores form normative samples of college students who were similar in age, educational, and socioeconomic characteristics, as described by Gough and Heilbrun (1965) and Spielberger et al. (1970).

The ACL and the STAI were readministered two and one-half months later to 53 (37 males and 16 females) of the original respondents who were available for testing. No significant differences were found between the original scores of the 96 subjects from the original sample and the original scores of the 53 subjects from the retest subsample (Simmonds, 1977).

It is important to note that the two and one-half month period between testings represented a period of intensive resocialization for the residents. Given one purported major goal of this period at the farm, which was to train future group leaders and to strengthen the level of commitment of members to the organization's interpretation of Christian doctrine, it is reasonable to assume that members would describe themselves in a different manner at the end of their experience at the farm than they had at the beginning. For the most part, these members had been Christians for only a short time prior to the first testing. They had been chosen by the pastors of their branch houses to spend a three-month period of hard labor under primitive living conditions at the farm, a substantially different lifestyle from the mostly middle-class and relatively comfortable backgrounds experienced by most of these members sometime previously. The farm was isolated, and contact with outsiders was extremely limited. The authority of the pastors was nearly absolute, and members were required to follow strict rules limiting personal freedom. Interpersonal ties between regular members were very strong, and a compelling group norm prescribed that members "search their hearts" constantly for the "will of the Lord." Given these conditions, it might be assumed that members would begin to describe themselves in terms similar to those of the normative group over time, since the religious group strongly encouraged members to subscribe to many of the values found within the dominant society, such as the value of work, obeying the law, the sanctity of marriage, personal stability, and productive interpersonal relations.

RESULTS

Table 1 shows t-test comparisons between members of this religious group and the normative sample of college students. Significance levels are shown at the .001 level of significance, since a lower level (e.g., .01 or .05) would have shown significant differences on nearly every variable. Scores for the Jesus move-

Simmonds / CONVERSION OR ADDICTION [121]

ment group were significantly higher than were those of the normative group on the ACL variables of unfavorable adjectives checked, succorance, and counseling-readiness, while they were significantly lower on the variables of defensiveness, a favorable adjectives checked, self-confidence, self-control, personal adjustment, achievement, dominance, endurance, order, intraception, nurturance, affiliation, heterosexuality, change, and number of adjectives checked. Trait anxiety scores on the STAI were also found to be significantly higher for the religious sample, although state anxiety scores were not significantly different. These

TABLE 1
Comparisons of Differences Between Means for
96 Jesus Movement Subjects and a Normative Sample

ACL VARIABLE:	Values of t:
Defensiveness	-5.80*
Favorable Adjectives Checked	-8.72*
Unfavorable Adjectives Checked	4.13*
Self-confidence	-10.18*
Self-control	-6.83*
Lability	-1.08
Personal Adjustment	-6.83*
Achievement	-8.76*
Dominance	-8.94*
Endurance	-6.08*
Order	-7.33*
Intraception	-6.95*
Nurturance	-4.15*
Affiliation	-4.96*
Heterosexuality	-5.13*
Exhibition	-1.17
Autonomy	-1.54
Aggression	.13
Change	-6.36*
Succorance	7.34*
Abasement	2.34
Deference	.92
Counseling-readiness	4.57*
Number of Adjectives Checked	-8.32*
STAI:	
Trait Anxiety	10.98*
State Anxiety	3.07

NOTE: A negative value of t denotes lower scores for the religious sample than for the normative sample.
*Significant at the .001 level of significance for a two-tailed test.

dramatic differences between the two groups were very similar to results obtained from another group of members of this organization, as reported by Simmonds et al. (1976).

Rather than inspecting each of these personality variables separately, it is perhaps more useful to examine the pattern of the profiles for the religious group in general. According to descriptions of each variable offered by Gough and Heilbrun (1965) and by Spielberger et al. (1970), the religious sample's scores fell in a negative or "maladaptive" direction on each variable for which there was a significant difference. It is important to note that while these profiles were probably not "maladaptive" with reference to the group context, they were "maladaptive" if patterns found within the dominant society are used as a referent (see Simmonds et al., 1976, for more discussion of this point).

Table 2 shows the degree of difference in each of the personality variables between pre- and posttests for the 53 subjects who could be located after the two and one-half month interval. None of the variables showed any significant longitudinal differences. Despite the fact that members lived in an isolated, authoritarian environment which purported to strengthen the degree of the members' commitments to Christian beliefs, there is no evidence of personality change across time in this group. As noted previously, however, there are methodological considerations which may have accounted for this lack of change.

These members were tested *after* conversion to fundamentalist Christianity, but, based on questionnaire data obtained at the same time as the personality scores, it seems reasonable to assume that preconversion personality scores, had they been available, would have resulted in similar "maladaptive" profiles. For instance, the respondents were asked about their use of drugs, alcohol, and tobacco prior to conversion. The self-reported data indicated that 87 (91%) had used alcohol, that 73 (76%) had smoked tobacco, and that 93 (97%) had used drugs prior to conversion. In accord with severe proscriptions against the use of these substances within the group, the self-reported frequency of use of these agents was virtually nil at the time of the survey. A large number—37 (40%)—of the members had been users of opiates (e.g., herion and the like) prior to conversion, and a great many more were heavy users of other "addictive" drugs

TABLE 2
Comparisons of Differences between Means of
Pretest and Posttest Administrations for 53 Subjects

ACL VARIABLE:	Values of t:
Defensiveness	-.17
Favorable Adjectives Checked	.39
Unfavorable Adjectives Checked	-.49
Self-confidence	.60
Self-control	.66
Lability	-1.13
Personal Adjustment	.10
Achievement	.13
Dominance	.56
Endurance	-.23
Order	.27
Intraception	-.22
Nurturance	.24
Affiliation	1.38
Heterosexuality	.67
Exhibition	.31
Autonomy	.86
Aggression	-.41
Change	1.06
Succorance	-.41
Abasement	-1.25
Deference	.41
Counseling-readiness	-.77
Number of Adjectives Checked	-.88
STAI:	
Trait Anxiety	-1.80
State Anxiety	-.46

NOTE: Negative values of t denote higher posttest than pretest scores.

such as amphetamines and barbiturates. Furthermore, the frequency of drug usage was very high. Fifty-five of the 93 drug users took drugs once a day or more, and 29 used drugs once a week or more, but less than once a day. Only six reported that they used drugs less than once a week, but more than once a month.

Other evidence indirectly supports this description of "maladaptivity" or dependency prior to conversion. Over half of the members (50) reported that they had had trouble with the law prior to conversion, and 35 had seen a psychologist or psychiatrist in a therapeutic context. Forty-four of the residents had thought seriously about suicide, and 18 of these had actually made suicide attempts. Only 13 of the residents reported that their level of life satisfaction had been neutral or unhappy, with the majority of this number (47) reporting that their lives had been very unhappy.

The pattern which emerges from these findings is one of "maladaptivity," which is suggestive of the dependency profiles described earlier. Essentially, these converts were tested at three points in time: (1) prior to conversion through retrospective questionnaire data, (2) shortly after conversion through personality tests, and then (3) after a period of intensive resocialization within the group, again with the same personality tests. At all three points, the notion of dependency is suggested.

CONCLUSIONS

This is not a tightly controlled experiment, and, until it is possible to test members of this or another such group under different conditions, no definitive conclusions can be drawn. The pattern which has emerged from these data, however, suggests that these converts showed personality profiles which were radically different from those of a normative comparison sample, and that, across time in the group during an intensive resocialization experience, there was no evidence of the personality change which might have been expected to occur.

It has not been possible to test these subjects both prior to and following conversion to this Jesus movement organization, simply because it was not known who would be likely to join or where to find these people even if they seemed to be likely candidates for conversion. There is some evidence to suggest, however, that most of these people may not have undergone the radical change in personality which is implied by usual definitions of conversion. It is possible that these people may not have been experiencing a conversion from one central behavioral system to another, but that they were simply finding another environment or belief system which was more consistent with their needs. In other words, affiliation with a Jesus movement group may represent a continuation of the same basic psychological patterns held by these people before they joined the group.

Since religious people seem to be describable in terms of relatively high levels of dependence, as noted earlier, it seems useful to borrow a concept suggested by Peele and Brodsky (1975)—that of "addiction." According to these writers, *addiction* is

> a person's attachment to a sensation, an object, or another person . . . such as to lessen his appreciation of and ability to deal with other things in his environment, or in himself, so that the has become increasingly dependent on that experience as his only source of gratification.

Applying this idea to conversion in the Jesus movement suggests that a member is simply "switching" from her/his former source of gratification (e.g., drugs) to another, "the Lord." This is an adaptive response for a person who does not believe that s/he has an internal capacity to deal with the normal frustrations of life. Rather than developing these internal capabilities when one form of external dependency is not fulfilling her/his needs, the person seeks an alternative source of gratification which appears to meet her/his needs. Jesus movement groups provide a stable, meaningful, and traditional belief system, close friendships, work, food, and shelter. In the sense that these believers adopt a lifestyle which differs substantially from the one that they previously had, then "conversion" is an appropriate concept to describe this change. The data from Table 1, however, which implies substantial personality differences for these religious converts in comparison with a normative sample, as well as the data from Table 2, which indicates no significant personality change across time in the group, brings into question this conceptualization of "conversion." It seems likely that members of the group may be perpetuating personality patterns which they had held prior to affiliation and which do not appear to be any more "adaptive" following affiliation or after some experience in the group. In this case, "addiction" might be a more useful conceptual description of the experience of members of the Jesus movement.

Peele and Brodsky (1975) imply that the addictive personality is one who lacks confidence to deal with life independently. S/he is fearful, a highly anxious person, low in self-confidence, and ready to rely on larger forces such as counseling, institutions, other people, drugs, or belief systems which can provide her/him with protection. "Disbelieving his own adequancy, recoiling from challenge, the addict welcomes control from outside himself as the ideal state of affairs" (Peele and Brodsky, 1975: 60). Based on the ACL and STAI results obtained from the sample of religious converts, it seems reasonable to infer that members of the sample in general could be described in terms of the *addictive personality*.

Peele and Brodsky say that many addicts find little difficulty in switching from one addiction to another. Their brief description of the addictive elements of conversion to a Jesus movement belief system is appropriate for the group under study here: "the denial of past and future, the release from anxiety and effort, the evasion of sexual maturity, the unassailable group ideology" (Peele and Brodsky, 1975: 168). For group members who have experienced a great deal of personality difficulty in their lives prior to conversion and who have already been exposed to some addictive patterns, the switch to Jesus is often quite attractive. The group espouses the idea of "being born again in Jesus," of negating all previous life experiences, and of dedicating all present life experiences to the Lord. Furthermore, the importance of the self is denied. Everything is done under the "direction of" and "for the Lord." Any activity hinting of self-assertion is condemned by group ideology as being "willful" or "vain." Little personal freedom is experienced by the new convert; s/he is under the authoritarian rule of a pastor, and only after a member has spent considerable time in the group and attained some level of leadership can s/he begin to exert more personal freedom.

Anecdotal evidence gathered suggests that the switching of addictions is easily accomplished. Many daily users of heroin, of alcohol, and of tobacco said that the great fulfillment that they experienced from "knowing the Lord" made withdrawal from these agents a very easy task. The group's strictures against masturbation and other premarital sexual experiences presented problems for many residents, but "through prayer and faith" the residents reported that their "belief in the Lord" helped to overcome these desires. In general, the "high" that these members had experienced through other means prior to conversion was easily replaced by being "high on the Lord" (see Adams and Fox, 1972).

When they were asked how happy their lives were now in the group, 95 reported that they were happy (one resident gave a neutral response). When they were asked how well they got along with other members of the group, 94 gave positive responses, and only two answered neutrally. None of the residents indicated any unhappiness or that they were experiencing poor relationships with other members of the community. Of course, any interpretation of these data must take into account the tendency of people to justify to themselves and to others a commitment that they have made, especially when the others are a group of "non-believing" researchers.

Thus, although it is impossible to draw final conclusions about applying the concept of addiction to the Jesus movement, the idea appears to merit futher research. Conversion was originally a lay term, an everyday concept, which was employed to describe the radical change which a person goes through when making a commitment to a new religious belief system, and it is frequently accompanied by a euphoric behavioral response. Use of this term carries overtones of rationalization or justification for the religious commitment, as if to imply that life prior to conversion had been evil, sinful, and fraught with personal difficulty, while life after conversion is happy, secure, and sure to lead to eternal salvation. This conceptualization of conversion has been adopted by most social scientists, and they retain the assumption that there must be a radical change in the person making such a religious commitment. Evidence from this Jesus movement group, however, suggests (although not definitively) that perhaps there is no radical change in personality either at the point of "conversion" or after experience in the group. Members may be clinging to an external source of gratification, similar to ones that they had searched for prior to affiliation with the group. In this sense, conversion may represent nothing more than a different context in which to perpetuate their addictive search for security.

REFERENCES

ADAMS, R.L. and R. J. FOX (1972) "Mainlining Jesus: the new trip." Society 9: 50-56.
BLACK, M. S. and P. LONDON (1966) "The dimension of guilt, religion, and personal ethics." J. of Social Psychology 69: 39-54.

DUKE, J. D. (1964) "Placebo reactivity and tests of suggestibility." J. of Personality 32: 227-236.

FISHER, S. (1964) "Acquiescence and religiosity." Psych. Reports 15: 784.

GLOCK, C. Y. (1964) "The role of deprivaiton in the origin and evolution of religious groups," pp. 24-36 in R. Lee and M. E. Marty (eds.) Religion and Social Conflict. New York: Oxford Univ. Press.

GOLDSEN, R. K., M. ROSENBERG, R. M. WILLIAMS, and E. A. SUCHMAN (1960) What College Students Think. Princeton, NJ: Van Nostrand.

GORDON, D. F. (1974) "The Jesus people: an identity synthesis." Urban Life and Culture 3: 159-178.

GOUGH, H. G. (1952) The Adjective Check List. Palo Alto, CA: Consulting Psychologists Press.

——— and A. B. HEILBRUN (1965) The Adjective Check List Manual. Palo Alto, CA: Consulting Psychologists Press.

HARDER, M. W. (1974) "Sex roles in the Jesus movement." Social Compass 21: 345-353.

——— J. T. RICHARDSON, and R. B. SIMMONDS (1976) "Life style: sex roles, courtship, marriage and family in a changing Jesus movement organization." Int. Rev. of Modern Sociology 6: 155-172.

——— (1972) "Jesus people." Psychology Today 6 (December): 45ff.

MAUSS, A. L. and D. W. PETERSEN (1974) "Les 'Jesus freaks' et le retour a la respectabilite." Social Compass 21: 269-281.

PEELE, S. and A. BRODSKY (1975) Love and Addiction. New York: Taplinger.

RICHARDSON, J. T., R. B. SIMMONDS, and M. W. HARDER (1975) "The evolution of a Jesus movement organization." Paper presented at the annual meeting of the American Sociological Association, San Francisco.

RICHARDSON, J. T., M. W. STEWART, and R. B. SIMMONDS (1977) Organized Miracles: A Study of a Communal Youth Fundamentalist Group. (forthcoming)

ROBBINS, T. (1969) "Eastern mysticism and the resocialization of drug users: the Meher Baba cult." J. for the Scientific Study of Religion 8: 308-317.

SIMMONDS, R. B. (1977) "The people of the Jesus movement: a personality assessment of members of a fundamentalist religious community." Ph.D. dissertation, University of Nevada.

——— (1976a) "Addiction and the Jesus movement." Paper presented at the annual meeting of the Society for the Scientific Study of Religion, Philadelphia.

——— (1976b) "Jesus people: conversion or addiction?" Paper presented at the annual meeting of the Association for the Sociology of Religion, New York.

——— J. T. RICHARDSON, and M. W. HARDER (1976) "A Jesus movement group: an adjective check list assessment." J. for the Scientific Study of Religion 15: 323-337.

——— (1974) "Organizational aspects of a Jesus movement community." Social Compass 21: 269-281.

SPIELBERGER, C. D. (1968) The state-trait anxiety inventory. Palo Alto, CA: Consulting Psychologists Press.

——— R. L. GORSUCH, and R. E. LUSHENE (1970) State-Trait Anxiety Inventory Manual. Palo Alto, CA: Consulting Psychologists Press.

WALTERS, O. S. (1957) "The religious background of fifty alcoholics." Q. J. of the Study of Alcohol 18: 405-416.

The Catholic Charismatic Renewal movement is the focus of this paper, which offers an insightful analysis of one group's attempt to become glossolalic. Special attention is given to the crucial role of leadership and the reaction of external church authorities.

Searching for Surrender

A Catholic Charismatic Renewal Group's Attempt to Become Glossolalic

FRANCES R. WESTLEY
McGill University

This paper is a study of the ritual of sharing and the process of commitment in a small Catholic Charismatic Renewal movement. The Catholic Charismatic Renewal movement (CCR) is an anomaly—a Pentacostal revival within, not separate from, the most traditional and ritualistic of Christian churches. It offers the phenomena of middle-class people speaking in tongues and experiencing possession trances as they receive the "Baptism of the Spirit." This paper examines one CCR group whose members tried, but failed, to attain this special experience.

BACKGROUND OF THE MOVEMENT

The Catholic Charismatic Renewal movement originated in the mid-sixties in the United States. Apparently an outgrowth of

Author's Note: *This paper was presented to the Canadian Society for the Study of Religion, Quebec City, 1976.*

FRANCES R. WESTLEY received her B.A. in English Literature from Middlebury College in Vermont. She received an M.A. in Sociology from McGill University in 1975 and is currently enrolled in a doctoral program in the Department of Sociology at McGill University.

[129]

the "Cursillo" (little course) movement and an aftermath of the liberalizing effect of Vatican II, the CCR represented for many Catholics a chance to revitalize their faith and their lives. As one priest put it:

> After Vatican II a lot of changes took place . . . a lot of-people were upset, they felt that something was missing. [There was] a need for renewal. It came at a time when people were hungry . . . some priests and lay people needed something extra to keep them going.

In 1966, at the national Cursillo conference, a young philosophy student named Stephen Clark introduced a book by a Protestant Pentacostal minister, David Wilkerson (1963), *The Cross and the Switchblade*. This book was a testimony of faith in the Spirit, by which Wilkerson lived. He looked for and saw the will of God in his most basic decisions—even how to find his way in a strange city. With the help of the Spirit, Wilkerson claimed to have performed miracles, bringing street gangs in New York City to the ways of God. Catholic Cursillo leaders were so impressed by this evidence of the rewards of faith and its effect on the experience of everyday living that they invited some Pentacostal ministers to meet and pray with them. Soon Catholics began receiving the gifts of the Spirit, including the all-important Baptism in the Spirit which included the gift of tongues or glossolalia.

In this notion of a direct individual relationship with God, the Catholic Charismatic Renewal movement departs from Catholicism, even the more liberal Catholicism of Vatican II.

Nevertheless, the movement has been tacitly accepted by the Catholic Church. It is housed in parish halls and often led by parish priests, while Catholic theologians struggle to reconcile the two philosophies. This is aided by the fact that members themselves show great eagerness to effect such a reconciliation. Studies (Fichter, 1975; McGuire, 1974, 1975; Harrison, 1974) have shown that the majority of members of the CCR were ardent Catholics before joining the movement. They have no intention of leaving the church; rather, they hope to bring the church to the movement. They are succeeding to the extent that an estimated 25,000 members attended a recent CCR conference in 1974.

Particularly interesting for sociologists is that the CCR movement defies the economic deprivation arguments usually applied to sects and cults of this type. Among the Protestant Pentacostal movements, new sects have tended to fit the traditional pattern, appealing to lower-income groups. However, the CCR is predominantly a middle-class movement (Fichter, 1975; McGuire, 1974, 1975; Harrison, 1974). This fact is particularly significant for the study of conversion and "surrender to the Spirit," which is central to the charismatic experience. Such "bridge-burning" acts, as Gerlach and Hine (1970) have noted, are sometimes marked by possession trances and often by glossolalia. Hence, they are not easily accessible to middle-class adherents.

> To surrender oneself without benefit of alcohol to the excesses of uncontrolled articulation and possible involuntary motor activity and to cap such indignities by calling it possession by the Holy Spirit, is, by middle class American standards, indecent if not immoral or insane. [Gerlach and Hine, 1970: 25][1]

RESEARCH AND METHODOLOGY

This paper examines the commitment process in a small CCR group in the Montreal area. Members of this group to date have not managed to make the complete "surrender" of which Gerlach and Hine spoke. Nevertheless, the process leading to commitment and surrender is evident in weekly meetings. It involves a gradual reinterpretation of experience and a shifting of responsibility from self to others. It begins with a ritual called "sharing" and ends, ideally, with the complete surrender of self. However, this paper will suggest that the surrender which is experienced as a spiritual relinquishing of self-control, a surrender of self to a higher power, is in fact duplicated on a social level by the surrender of self to the direction and protection of the group. The focus will be on the ritual of sharing—first to indicate how it leads to such shifting of responsibility, and second to suggest that the ritual itself must be controlled and focused if it is to have the desired result of attaining spiritual surrender.

The data for this paper were gathered over a three-month period during which the researcher attended weekly group meetings and conducted unstructured interviews with members on an informal basis. Members knew that the researcher was doing work of a sociological nature, but they assumed as well that her interest was personal and that she was a possible convert. At the time of the study, the group had been in existence for about six years and had a membership of eight, with occasional attendance of three other people. It was housed in the parish of St. K. in a church basement and was led by a priest who was marginally connected to the parish. All the members were women—except for one boy, a son of a member and a priest— and all but one were over 35. Only two members, Pearl and Gary, had "gifts": Pearl the gift of "healing" and Gary that of "tongues." Most members, including the priest, attended the much larger neighboring English CCR group at St. A. This latter group, which St. K. members saw as a model, had a much more formal, highly organized structure, and its members had a high incidence of gifts—particularly that of tongues.

THE PROCESS OF COMMITMENT—
SHIFTING RESPONSIBILITY

In discussing what changes the group has effected, one member described a change in the leader:

> Father N. is not the same Father N. I knew two years ago. He is 100% charismatic—he was very shy, very reserved, and now he is open, so beautiful.

This change marked the experience of several of the members and was often referred to as the ability to share. Learning to share was not only seen as an important part of becoming a charismatic, it was at times expressed as the essence of charisma:

> We were never a charismatic group until Nov. 22. At the prayer meetings we had no one who would share. We would just kneel and pray. I think he [the leader] thought we were a hopeless group.

Sharing involved telling other members about life experiences, personal thoughts, hopes, and so on. At each meeting, Father N. would ask the group if anyone "had anything to share." He saw sharing as an important function, which the St. K. group fulfilled. Individual members saw the moment that they began sharing as the moment of their rebirth. One woman felt that a weekend retreat wrought the important change for her:

> At the beginning of the weekend I told the Father that this isn't going to have any effect on me. I mean, I've been on cloud nine before. Up to Sunday afternoon nothing had happened to me. But then . . . on Thursday night they had a meeting and a lot of people got up to witness . . . there were some people there from St. A. . . . did anyone mention it [at the S. A. meeting]? Well, you know me for awhile . . . and I never say anything and I stood up . . . there must have been one hundred and fifty people there . . . and I wasn't nervous or anything. It's a once in a lifetime thing.

Father N. himself suggested that he had become more relaxed, less withdrawn, since "he began to share." He repeatedly asked the interviewer, "Perhaps there is something you'd like to share with the group," or he might, as he did in one case, simply announce:

> This is the moment when we can share our own lives with each other and today one member who has been very silent up to now is going to tell us what she's doing.

Sharing was, therefore, encouraged behavior. It seemed to be linked, on most people's part, to increased commitment to the group. It amounted to putting faith in others in the group and was rewarded by two closely linked group responses: prayer and healing.

TAKING RESPONSIBILITY FOR OTHERS

Requests for prayer followed closely on the heels of sharing. This desire for group support indeed seemed to motivate members to share:

> There's this man who I work with a lot—in the scout group on Fridays, at bowling Wednesday morning who I don't like . . . he really bugs me . . . help me to find Jesus in him . . . pray for me so I can forgive me.

At other times, members would support each other's prayers spontaneously. Brenda's employment situation became a "cause célebre" of the group. Pearl, in particular, prayed continually "for Brenda to get another job." Father N. himself often asked for prayers for his sick father and mentioned that, due to the relaxed personal quality of the group, he had felt greatly aided and supported by their prayers.

In addition to praying for each other, the group always would perform *group healings,* both mental and physical, for those members in need. These were, in general, led by Pearl, who was said to have the "gift of healing." If physical healing was needed, Pearl merely placed her hand over the injured area and prayed. However, if spiritual or mental healing—"probably the most important kind"—was necessary, Pearl would place her hands on the person's shoulders, and the group would gather around, placing their hands on Pearl or on the person to be healed. Thus, to the verbal support lent in prayer was given the reassurance of physical contact.

As a result of the members' sharing, their demands for prayer, and the increasing daily contact with each other, there was a rapid development of familiarity among group members. This expressed itself in informality, solicitude, frank curiosity, and equally frank advice. Members seemed to feel responsible for one another, as if they were a family. This attitude was especially encouraged by Father N., who saw it as an important part of the group experience. All members valued this sense of closeness: "I think we've put a lot of effort into these prayer meetings. We're like one family now."

There was a continual indication that this group support was in fact important to members and helped them to change their behavior, as typified by the following statement:

> I wanted to tell the group . . . you know last week I asked for prayers because of that man I couldn't forgive . . . well the next time I saw the man all the wounds just went out of my heart and I saw Christ in him. I forgave him in Christ. I never realized Father N. is always saying there is power in small groups . . . but I never realized how powerful prayer in such a small group can be.

This last quote indicates the third element of shifting responsibility which goes on in the charismatic group. Not only do members assume responsibility for each other, but they relinquish responsibility for themselves.

RELINQUISHING SELF-RESPONSIBILITY

Learning to become a charismatic involves a considerable relinquishing of self-control. As pointed out earlier, sharing involves dropping certain inhibitions, opening one's inner thoughts and attitudes for redefinition in terms of charismatic beliefs.

Initially members seem to rely on others, more experienced, to provide the interpretation:

> Brenda: Something happened to me . . . I never say nothing to my boss because I'm afraid . . . and the other day my boss says I think I'm getting a new customer and I say, "Oh really, you gettin' a new customer, how about raisin' my pay?" And he said, "Oh no" . . . but even though he said no . . . I still had the courage to ask anything before and I told Emilie, and she said that it was the Spirit.
>
> Barbara: Sure, it was the Holy Spirit working in you, Brenda. . . . He wants you to be brave.

However, as time passes and members become more accomplished sharers, they begin to provide their own reinterpretations of experience. These reinterpretations fall generally into three categories: events are seen as controlled by "divine direction," "divine intervention," and "manifestations of the Spirit."

In the first case, the "Lord's direction" is actively sought or a message is claimed—as in the case of Pearl, who saw a telephone call as a message from the Lord to go on:

> This week I was very low . . . I didn't go out all week . . . and I said Lord what do you mean for me . . . I thought it was all over. . . . Then the phone rang . . . it was my friend   . Her mother was dying; she's very old and wouldn't let the priest come to give her last rites . . . so I prayed with her that the priest could come and the very next day her mother asked for the priest and I thought "Lord, you're telling me to go on . . . because I was really low, you know . . . I didn't think I could go on . . . and then he gave me a sign.

In other cases, events are seen as direct intervention by God (divine intervention) on the actor's behalf:

> At one point during the "witnessing" Gary told the following story: I have a friend who has a beautiful cross and I wanted a cross . . . I went to several stores around but I couldn't find one. So I prayed and said, Lord I want something to wear to show I belong to you—if you want me to have it I know you'll bring it to me somehow. Then a friend of mine at St. Augustine's came to visit me . . . I had been praying for a cross. . . . And when he left he said I've left something for you on the hall table and when I opened the box I found this cross and I couldn't believe it, so praise be to Jesus.

Events involving manifestations of the Spirit were interpreted as evidence of the "will of God." These events are answers to prayers never consciously formulated—they are witness to God's concern for the individual's welfare:

> God is really good to me. He takes care of me. . . . I was sort of down that evening and was thinking hard, not paying much attention to what was going on when all this started [a drug addict at St. A. started disrupting the meeting and the priest performed an exorcism] three of my friends gathered around me so I wouldn't see . . . they were protecting me because they didn't want me to see.

A very interesting consistency emerges in these miracle tales and reinterpretations: they generally involve not only the actor, but other members who have prayed for the actor. In the above case, the concern of fellow members to protect Pearl from something they knew would offend her is seen as God's good care.

The member who brought Gary the cross was undoubtedly aware, if not of the specific prayer, of Gary's depression and uncertainty and his need for a symbol to identify with at this time. His visit brought the reaffirmation that was needed.

In sum, it is interesting to note that, as members assume responsibility for each other, it becomes increasingly possible for individuals to eschew personal responsibility and to view the events of their lives in a larger context in which the assumption is made that they will be directed and cared for by a Divine Spirit who shapes their lives.

SUMMARY

The charismatic group at St. K. provided a special experience for members. This experience depended upon the members' ability to share. Once personal material in the form of prayers, hopes, and ideas is presented to the group, a reinterpretation begins for the individual. The group becomes responsible for the individual, caring and supporting him/her. Increasingly, the individual's life is seen as directed and touched by God. In turn, his or her purpose comes to be defined as caring for others and as contributing individual gifts toward the operation of the group and "in praise of the Lord."

Beyond these evident rewards, none of the members at St. K. had experienced at the time of this writing the ecstatic trances which mark the Baptism of the Holy Spirit in the group at St. A. and many other CCR groups. These trances can be seen as the ultimate "bridge-burning act," which precedes total commitment to a group. No doubt this "surrender" is the end-product of the process of reinterpretation and shifting responsibility described at St. K. It may be hypothesized that increasing commitment and breakdown of inhibitions on the part of the individual go hand-in-hand with group support and reinterpretation of experience until the individual is prepared to take the final leap and "allow the Holy Spirit to take possession of them" and to speak through them in tongues. It may also be hypothesized that this increasing relinquishing of self-responsibility and control, so satisfying for charismatics, may be a reflection of a preexisting sense of helplessness and impotence. Certainly the members of St. K. were not people who exercised much control over their destinies. There is little doubt that the group allowed them to relinquish responsibility for that which they already could not control.

The question remains why members and the group at St. K. as a whole failed to move to the ecstatic trance stage, failed to receive tongues or witness miracles in their midst, failed to break down those final inhibitions. We will attempt to answer this question in the remaining section of this paper.

FAILURE TO SURRENDER

Despite the obvious gratifications which the members of St. K. felt, there was among them a sense of failure. "There's something wrong with this group" seemed to be the consensus. The explanations for it were varied, but centered on the disunity and tension often evident in prayer meetings. This tension was felt to be nonspiritual, anticharismatic, and even "the work of the devil" by many members. Behind the disunity lay a series of interrelated factors, but at the crux of the problem lay, once again, the ritual of sharing. It was the way in which this ritual was performed which seemed to dictate whether a particular meeting was viewed as a success or a failure.

UNCONTROLLED SHARING

Father N. summed up the March 21 meeting as follows:

This meeting has been about joys and sorrows . . . of course associated with the death and resurrection of Christ . . . there has been some sorrow but this is the most joyous meeting I have ever seen here. . . . I think we should praise the Lord . . . the Spirit has been with us.

To say that "the Spirit is with us" is high praise for a charismatic meeting. However, the preceding week, Father N. had felt it necessary to interrupt the meeting continually and finally to bring it to a halt altogether:

After this final distraction, Father N. suggests "we pray in silence." He inhales deeply during the silence. "I felt there was a tension, that everyone was tense . . . I felt we needed a moment of silence."

Father N. left the group because he felt too much tension, and stated that tension "did not come from the Holy Spirit"—he viewed tension and the Holy Spirit as diametrically opposed.

The difference in these two meetings centers around the "sharing" or "witnessing," as other elements—prayers, hymns, and scripture readings—remained constant. The successful meeting took place the week before Easter, and the group members' minds seemed to be on the resurrection. Laura began the meeting by reading the passion and by talking very personally of how Jesus must have felt in the garden. Gary sang a song he had composed himself about the death of Christ and "witnessed" about how the group's prayers had wrought a change in him: "I never realized how powerful prayer in such a small group can be." This brought an enthusiastic witness from Pearl about how the Lord had guided her, and one from Laura about how Jesus had "cooled off" a man who had been persecuting her.

On the other hand, at the meeting the week before, Pearl had been totally silent and Gary was absent. Laura had chosen to talk about a story from St. Paul about a man who had fallen out a window. Joan had launched into sharing the story of her court case, and Brenda shared the difficulties of her job. These sharings were notable because they made no mention of God or the Holy Spirit. This was in sharp contrast to the week before, when all witnessing of experience indicated God as the director of events.

At most meetings, Pearl and Gary embroidered their sharing with mention of God or the Spirit. (Recall that these are the two laymen who are perceived as having "gifts"—Pearl with healing, Gary with "tongues.") With Pearl silent and Gary absent, sharing became secular and on the level of a group therapy session. Why does this happen?

PROBLEM OF CHARISMA

It is evident that sharing in the approved manner is a question partly of initiation and partly of social control. The latter question depends largely on leadership. Father N., as we have noted, was a reluctant leader. He felt that the role of the priest was "to discern the devil . . . who will try to disturb the meeting . . . all kinds of human problems need to be purified."

Nevertheless, he did not see himself as particularly adept at social control. He went to St. A., he said, because he learned a lot from Father V. (the leader at St. A.) about how to handle such situations. However, it was obvious from his nervous and tentative interruptions that he was not at ease with policing the meetings. Father V., on the other hand, made no bones about cutting-off anyone "disturbing" a meeting.

Perhaps, more importantly, Father N. was not a convinced charismatic himself. He had no gifts such as tongues, healing, or prophecy, and he was not even convinced of their validity. Asked about Pearl's gift, he responded: "it's something I'm not too sure of . . . she prays for people and people are healed . . . they feel better . . . it could be autosuggestion." In the meetings he would often turn to Pearl and ask her to witness when the meeting lagged, seeming to depend upon her certainty in the presence of the Spirit. After Gary joined the group, Father N. turned the choice of hymns over to him (a task jealously guarded by Father V.) and followed Gary's lead in raising his hands skyward during hymns, a gesture Father N. had never made alone.

Father N.'s uncertainty about elements of charismatic renewal was reflected by other members of the group. In all, there was evidence of a need for the kind of indoctrination that went on at St. A., and members talked wistfully of getting help from St. A.:

> what we need is to get some pentacostals to come and visit us and show us how to do it . . . there's a couple who gives seminars to St. A. Maybe they could come and give one here.

It is difficult to establish causal links, but it is evident that the dissension over charisma, the lack of "gifted" laymen, and the weak leadership all contributed to the failure of the group to maintain the kind of high spiritual level they felt at the March 21 meeting. In addition, the inability of the group to increase in numbers was directly linked to the opposition of the pastor at St. K.—Father R.—to the group in general.

HOSTILITY OF CHURCH AUTHORITIES

Father R. was opposed to the charismatic group. Father N. suggested that "many of the priests didn't approve of the C.R." and that even the Bishop who was in charge of the renewal movement for the Montreal area thought of charismatics as "a bunch of kooks." Accordingly, Father R. never mentioned the St. K. prayer meeting in the bulletin or at regular mass. Needless to say, this cut down on recruits and made Father N. very uncomfortable. However, in addition to the fact that the charismatic beliefs did not interest Father R., this particular group aggravated him further by continually causing internal strife in the church. Before Father N. took over, as previously mentioned, an argument had caused so much commotion that he had threatened to throw them out: "Father R. said . . . no more fights . . . they were fed up with charismatics. Father R. thought fights were charismatic."

During the meeting prior to the one at which Father N. resigned, Pearl had again gone complaining to Father R. that the prayer sheets had been vandalized. She caused so much trouble that Father R. pressured the already ambivalent Father N. to leave. ("I just get a feeling from those upstairs . . . maybe the group shouldn't continue.") Father N. felt that the size of the group was largely to blame, that dissension could be avoided by joining the larger group: "In a bigger group we just wouldn't notice these things, these personal things." Implicit in this remark was the final factor contributing to the sense of failure—the presence of St. A. as an inescapable model.

COMPARISON TO ST. A.

Comparison of St. A. and St. K. was a continuous part of the meetings at St. K. Usually St. K. compared unfavorably:

> some [hymns] were abandoned because the group couldn't carry the tune. "You really need an accompaniment," said Father N., "at St. A. they have a ministry of music."

St. A. was generally recognized as a model for charismatic meetings. Father N. often read from Father V.'s book on charismatic meetings, using it as a guideline for the St. K. meetings. Father N. greatly admired Father V. and felt he "learned a lot" from him. Other St. K. members envied St. A. because they spoke in tongues, had so large a group, had teaching sessions and were in general "more advanced": "St. A. is at a higher spiritual level . . . it's just a question of people . . . they have the gift of tongues and the gift of prophecy."

Most members attended St. A. and had important social connections there. They continued to cling to St. K., however, primarily (according to Father N.) because the group was small, democratic, and everyone had a chance to share—unlike St. A., which was more anonymous. However, it was also this small size, as we have noted, which was held responsible for the sense of failure: "In small groups, if personal problems become too big . . . there is disunity, disharmony . . . it is best to disband and let the group join a bigger group." In sum, small groups promote sharing, and sharing personal problems was perceived of as the first step toward becoming a charismatic. However, "personal problems" also arise in small groups and may cause the downfall of such a group.

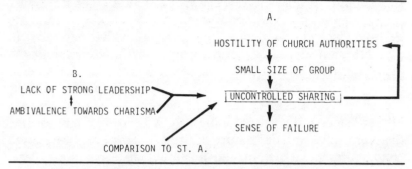

Figure 1: Interrelationship of Factors Contributing to a Sense of Failure among Members of St. K.

SUMMARY

We have now come full circle in what amounts to a cluster of factors affecting each other and contributing to a sense of failure. Although causal links can only be hypothesized, these factors seem to interrelate in the pattern shown in Figure 1.

As evident in this figure, the factors cluster in two groups linked by "uncontrolled sharing." In the first cluster, "A," it appears that the hostility of church authorities results in a failure of the group to grow (as it is not publicized, indeed, repressed). The small size in turn results, it is claimed, in uncontrolled sharing, and prayer meetings usually degenerate into, at best, group therapy sessions and, at worst, group squabbles. This dissension in turn results in increased hostility of authorities, who see the charismatics as troublemakers.

In the second cluster, "B," it appears that the weak leadership of Father N. leads to ambivalence and confusion concerning the ideals and the definition of the group (while Father N.'s own ambivalence to charisma makes his leadership weak). These two variables also contribute to uncontrolled sharing, as social control such as that at St. A. is lacking. Finally, comparison to St. A., a large, accepted group with a clear sense of its ideals and a strong leader, makes St. K. members acutely aware of the short-comings of their group.

Hence, we see that "uncontrolled sharing" is as important in the group's sense of failure as sharing in general is to the group's sense of purpose and success. The group at St. A., with its "higher spiritual level," does not permit every person the kind of intimate sharing which allows members of St. K. to involve themselves in each other's lives and establish a warm sense of community. On the other hand, the uncontrolled sharing at St. K. seems detrimental to the sense of participation in a spiritual movement, sacred and significant. In sum, it may be suggested that, with the proper leadership and acceptance, St. K.'s group might assume the more "charismatic" nature of St. A.'s. However, were those factors present, St. K. would no doubt also increase in size. Soon, organization and bureaucratization—"routinization" in Weber's terms—would be necessary, as it has already become at St. A. With increasing routinization, it is unlikely that the kinds of benefits we described in the first section of this paper will survive, based as they are on the "sharing" of each individual. St. K.'s group is smaller and lacks the organization and "charisma" characteristic of most CCR movements. Nevertheless, the group dynamics contain the seeds of the dilemma which must face all groups of the CCR (and, indeed, all charismatic movements). How does a group succeed in controlling and directing the sharing into the ritual channels which make the experience "spiritual" without, at the same time, destroying the therapeutic and familiar situation which, no doubt, accounts for the attraction of the group to most of its members? At the moment, the St. K. group is a CCR group without charisma. Nevertheless, the personal benefits it supplies for its small group of members has caused it to persist, and it may continue to do so.

REFERENCES

FICHTER, J. (1975) The Catholic Cult of the Paraclete. New York: Sheed & Ward.
GERLACH, L. P. and V. HINE (1970) People, Power, Change. New York: Bobbs-Merrill.
HARRISON, M. I. (1974) "Sources of recruitment to Catholic Pentacostalism." J. for the Scientific Study of Religion 13: 49-64.
McGUIRE, M. (1975) "Toward a sociological interpretation of the Catholic Pentacostal movement." Rev. of Religious Research 1975: 94-104.
——— (1974) "An interpretive comparison of elements of the Pentacostal and underground church movements in American Catholicism." Soc. Analysis 35: 57-65.
WILKERSON, D. (1963) The Cross and the Switchblade. Old Tappan, NJ: Fleming H. Revell Co., Spire Books.

This paper compares deprogramming with exorcism, thought reform, and resocialization, and offers insight into how members of the anticult movement justify their own involvement in "coercive conversion." It serves as a fitting, if ironic, close to this issue on conversion careers.

Deprogramming

The New Exorcism

ANSON D. SHUPE, Jr.
ROGER SPIELMANN
SAM STIGALL
University of Texas, Arlington

The mid-to-recent 1970s have witnessed a growing wave of sympathy among the courts and legislators for the apprehension, detention, and involuntary resocialization ("deprogramming") of persons belonging to such marginal religions as Hare Krishna, the Children of God, and Sun Myung Moon's Unification Church. The justification for such actions rests on the beliefs of many that these groups are gaining converts through a manipulative process of stressful conversion popularly known as "brainwashing"—hence, the converts do not act of their own free will or voluntary commitment. Under "temporary conservatorship" laws, designed for emergency situations when their irresponsibility might prove irreparably self-injurious, adults may be declared legally incompetent and forcibly held, with the approval of their "guardians," until the presumed effects of the given sect's or cult's influence are undone (i.e., until they recant their new

Authors' Note: *The authors wish to thank David Bromley, Joseph Ventimiglia, and Frank Weed for constructive criticisms of an earlier draft of this paper.*

ANSON D. SHUPE, Jr. is Assistant Professor of Sociology at the University of Texas at Arlington. His research and teaching interests are in the sociology of religion and comparative sociology. He is currently investigating parameters of the American anticult movement.

ROGER SPIELMANN is a graduate student in sociology at the University of Texas at Arlington. He is currently researching topics in sociolinguistics as well as in marginal religions.

SAM STIGALL is a graduate student in sociology at the University of Texas at Arlington. His current research interests include marginal religions and energy policy in the United States.

faith). In the meantime, the rights of the alleged "incompetent" to be legally represented and to contest this status in court can be suspended. Recently a tax-exempt organization called The Freedom of Thought Foundation, complete with "rehabilitation" ranch in Arizona, was established to conduct conservatorship-protected deprogrammings (Montagno, 1977).

The advent of this application of conservatorship laws has obvious societal implications for the freedom of religion. The state's willingness (with psychiatric cooperation) to consider attempts to distinguish "legitimate" religions from "illegitimate" ones[1] has been interpreted by some (Robbins, 1977; Knickerbocker, 1977) as a serious threat to civil liberties. The legitimacy of the process termed deprogramming (i.e., involuntary resocialization of cult members), directly or indirectly, has been associated with this controversy. The purpose of this paper is to report on those organizations currently advocating deprogramming and to examine their justifications for such reconversion. In doing so, we compare the phenomena of commitment to marginal religions and the deprogramming of persons so committed to demonic possession and exorcism, respectively. The latter are not intended as merely superficial analogies. Rather, the discernible similarity of assumptions and techniques may put current issues in a more relativist perspective. While a similar analogy to demonology has been suggested previously (Bauer, 1957) for communist thought control and indoctrination, the analogy has not yet been explored for marginal religious commitment and backlash.

METHODS

Data to support the generalizations asserted here have been gathered from a variety of sources. Since fall 1976, we have been involved in an ongoing investigation of the emerging anticult movement in North America (see Shupe, Spielmann, and Stigall, 1977) and have been in contact with national leaders of this movement.[2] Much of our information has derived from direct face-to-face or repeated telephone interviews with various groups' leaders as well as from the published literature of anticult groups, from mail-out questionnaires to their spokespersons, and, in one case,[3] from participant-observation of a national organization's headquarters. In addition, popular accounts of deprogramming (e.g., see Patrick and Dulack, 1976; Crittenden, 1976; Rasmussen, 1976) and interviews with eye-witnesses of deprogramming have been utilized.

In order to provide a background for discussing the deprogramming phenomenon, it may be useful to describe briefly the composition of anticult organizations (for a more extensive description, see Shupe, Spielmann, and Stigall, 1977). Most groups possess a fairly loose and informal structure, working with small budgets based on voluntary contributions. Their memberships can be typed into several general categories.

The largest category is made up of relatives and friends of persons who have joined marginal religious cults. The relatives are often parents, but may also include spouses. Their motives initially are twofold: first, to locate a particular cult member, and second, to persuade the member to leave the religious group. If the relatives are insistent, and if the member refuses to leave (or has previously refused), the next step may be to abduct the member against his or her will. Since many families perceive these marginal religions as exploitive and harmful, pursuit of the member (and the often mobile group) takes on a moral imperative. Conversely, the religious groups appear to appreciate the threat of this dogged determinism and serve to intensify the families' efforts by hiding, disguising, and isolating members.[4] While the return of a family member may signal the end of anticult involvement for some families, other families remain active in the movement. In many cases, a "functional autonomy" of involvement develops. The prolonged trauma of "losing" a family member, the efforts to "regain" that person, and the frequent adaptation of family lifestyle patterns to time-consuming anticult activities mean that anticultism becomes a powerful commitment not easily extinguished. This commitment may sustain continued involvement of the family long after a particular member has been recovered.[5]

The second category is made up of ex-cultists, including those who simply became disillusioned and those who themselves have undergone deprogramming. The latter type of ex-cultist is particularly apt to become an activist spokesperson due to the explicit negative reinterpretations of cult experiences gained during deprogramming. In addition, the emotional trauma surrounding the deprogramming experience and subsequent "return" to families appears to provide the foundation for strong personal commitment to anticult activists.

The third category consists of sympathetic sideliners whose involvement is typically more professional and less emotional. Such persons include psychiatrists, physicians, social workers, journalists, and sometimes social scientists. It may be that their services were at some time requested or that they gradually acquired a personal interest in marginal religions (e.g., Merritt, 1975). Occasionally they may have a professional or scientific interest in some aspect of cults (e.g., Clark, 1976). Though small in number, this type of member provides an extremely important legitimization function for the anticult movement. Such a person lends scientific credence to claims of "brainwashing" and "psychological enslavement," reinforcing the suspicions and fears of families. Such scientific legitimacy is an important component of the deprogramming rationale.

THE DEPROGRAMMING RATIONALE

The logic of deprogramming assumes the following: (1) that a person has experienced, through deception, hypnosis/drugs, or a lowering of normally resistant rationality by special techniques of deprivation, conversion to a new religious creed; (2) that after this conversion, the person is psychologically "enslaved" and is unable to act independently of a manipulator's directives; and (3) that a process reversal, or deprogramming of the "programmed" victim, is necessary to restore free will and rational choice. Since these faculties are fundamental elements of the American values of individual pursuit of happiness and personal growth, deprogramming takes on not only presumed therapeutic, but also moral, legitimacy.

Technically, however, anticultists do not regard the new religious commitment to marginal religious beliefs as the result of "true" conversion. Rather, due to the manipulative circumstances of the change in commitment, it represents a "pseudo-conversion." Explicitly rejecting the notion that deprogramming is resocialization (i.e., substituting one set of beliefs for another), West (1975: 1) reiterates this theme: "most of the cults whose members are subject to deprogramming were actually brainwashed rather than converted in the first place." Similarly, Merritt (1975: 3) states: "I strongly believe that the members are not exerting their own free will. Their free will has been given up to the whims of their leaders by the isolation, lack of sleep, sexual acts, poor eating and the sophistication of the psychological manipulations of the leaders. . . . The only comparisons that can be made with these groups, to help explain them, is to that of the Hitler Youth and the techniques used by the Chinese during what they call 're-education.' " Cult methods of recruitment and indoctrination, it is claimed, utilize methods similar to those employed by communist thought reformers on Korean and Vietnam prisoners of war. The gradual whittling away of critical thought processes is accomplished through persistent challenges to conventional religious beliefs that begin at an imperceptibly subtle level but which increase until the *naive* person is emotionally entrapped. This fact, coupled with strategically arranged fatigue, poor nutrition, little time for adequate reflection, and repetition of mesmerizing sounds or terms, disqualifies cult indoctrination from being resocialization.[6] In West's (1975: 2) words, cult "pseudo-conversion" involves "unthinking participation in group activities, a schedule designed to deprive followers of sleep, and a technique for short-circuiting reason through a conditioned reflex which is reinforced by group interaction."[7]

Because cult membership is believed to involve only "pseudo-conversion," anticultists maintain that the freedom of religious worship is not a relevant issue. Freedom of religion, as they interpret it, means the freedom to rationally and freely select the religion of one's preference. The conditions of "pseudo-conversion" therefore dissociate deprogramming from First Amendment considerations. In this way, anticultists perceive the apparent religious commitment of converts to marginal religious as actually representing "mind suppression," "psychological kidnapping," and "mental manipulation."

In addition, many anticult leaders seem conversant with the psychological literature on brainwashing published shortly after the Korean War (such as Lifton, 1963, 1957; Hunter, 1962, 1953; Sargent, 1957; Meerloo, 1956) and are aware of research on the effects of sensory-nutritional deprivation on suggestibility (see Biderman and Zimmer, 1961). They often point to the similarities between indoctrination/interrogation techniques of communist nations and the high pressure conditions of proselytization in cults such as the Children of God and the Unification Church.

Sympathetic professionals in the movement have offered evidence, however limited, that corroborates the "pseudo-conversion" perspective. For example, Clark (1976: 2-3), a psychiatrist, found that 15 of 27 cult members whom he examined (no details on the examination were provided) were either chronically schizophrenic or borderline personalities who sought conversion as "restitutive" or compensatory coping strategies. Clark distinguished between the "original" and the "imposed" personalities of cult members, the former being the normal product of socialization and maturation, the latter their temporary thought/behavior patterns established under cult influence. Deprogramming, Clark testified to a special investigating committee of the Vermont legislature (currently deliberating legislation to curtail cults), is thus a restoration process, an act (in his words) "of repersonalization."

By such arguments, anticultists justify the forced detention and deprogramming of cult members. Since cult members have surrendered their critical reasoning powers to others, there is little hope that they will drop out of their own conscious volition.[8] Literally, they are *possessed,* i.e., under the control of a separate personality or force that suppresses their own individual dispositions and uses them for purposes that they would normally not accept. Irrespective of the particular theory of demonology that may derive from a given theology, this phenomenology of attributed possession is not radically different from similar instances gleaned from the history of Christianity and other religions (see Keller, 1974; Robbins, 1974; Toner, 1974; Starkey, 1961). Other characteristics of the possessed, such as general physical debilitation, can be found in both historical and current cases.

DEPROGRAMMING AS EXORCISM

Thus far we have argued for the analogy between demonic possession and the brainwashing of cult members alleged by anticultists. In both cases, the victim is presumed beyond responsibility for his or her actions; when the influence of a third person or force is removed, the original personality and independent volition will be restored.

Nor is the analogy between deprogramming and exorcism a specious one. As support, we offer five characteristics of the exorcism rite that closely parallel deprogramming: purpose, characteristics of the exorcists/deprogrammers, duration, violence involved, and alternating threats and appeals.

PURPOSE

Exorcism can be defined as:

the act of driving, or warding off, demons or evil spirits, from persons, places or things, which are, or are believed to be, possessed or infested by them, or are liable to become victims or instruments of their malice. [Toner, 1974: 31]

In more contemporary jargon, West (1975: 2) claims:

Deprogramming aims at breaking the chains of fear, guilt, and repetitive thought, and at forcing evaluation of the unexamined beliefs that were injected into the victim's unresisting mind by the cult leaders after the behavioral chains were originally established. The process does not involve any alternative behavioral programming, but, rather, a dramatic, and hopefully, shocking presentation of alternative interpretations of specific phenomena.

In psychiatric terms, both processes attempt to restore normal ego-functioning. The emphasis in both is not on resocialization, but rather on the "liberation" of the possessed person. When possession is removed, the former "acceptable" personality will be free to manifest itself. In this sense, the deprogrammer is no more trying to convert the cult member than is the priest attempting, through the litany of the exorcism rite, to reconvert the person possessed by a demon. The priest addresses the demon, the deprogrammer (indirectly) challenges the influence of the cult.

CHARACTERISTICS OF EXORCISTS/DEPROGRAMMERS

The qualifications of exorcists in early Christianity resemble those of deprogrammers in the emerging American anticult movement.

In early Christianity, nonclerics and nonordained Christians could cast out demons in the name of the Holy Spirit. Only later, in the second and the third centuries, did exorcists become a specialty within the church hierarchy. Later, exorcism became a professional prerogative of those who had taken holy orders. Similarly, the first deprogrammer, Ted Patrick, had no special qualifications in psychology or psychiatry. The initial deprogrammings were essentially unstructured ad hoc affairs, without legal protection or more than a sense of urgency to guide the procedures.

More important, often those who have conducted or participated in exorcisms/deprogrammings have themselves experienced the respective "liberating" processes. Robbins (1974: 201) notes that during medieval outbreaks of demonic possession, exorcists tended to originate in the ranks of the previously possessed and exorcised. He quotes from the early eighteenth-century treatise, *L'Histoire des Diables de Loudun:* "exorcists almost all participate, more or less, in the effects of the demons, by vexations which they suffer from them, and few persons have undertaken to drive them forth who have not been troubled by them." Similarly, our informants in the anticult movement report that the most successful and enthusiastic deprogrammers are ex-cultists who have recently been deprogrammed. Better than others, they can empathize with the conflict experienced by cult members during the deprogramming. Part of their fervor may result from a wish for revenge against the cult. Their familiarity with cult doctrines may also aid the deprogrammer's attack on the given cult's claim to legitimacy, its inconsistencies, and so forth.

DURATION

Toner (1974: 4) mentions that in the case of a tenacious possession, repeated performance of the exorcism rite is sometimes necessary. Robbins (1974: 209) also comments that exorcism can prove a time-consuming ordeal.

Similarly, deprogramming is rarely accomplished without some lengthy effort for both cult member and deprogrammer(s). For example, Rasmussen (1976: 112) reports from his informants that the process often requires several days. Crittenden's (1976: 100) account of Ann Gordon's deprogramming mentions a third, and possibly fourth, day involved in her sessions at the hands of Ted Patrick. When one of our informants had his own daughter deprogrammed, he was relieved that it only required 12 hours.

The length of time involved in deprogramming is a function of this reconversion process' basic technique: argument. The efficacy of deprogramming rests in the deprogrammer debating inconsistencies in cult doctrines and behavior with the cult member, convincing the latter that they were deceived by cult leaders and had lost their "sense of reality" through exclusive exposure to cult perspectives. This sort of exchange, aided by the physical and psychic strains on cult members, can only occur if they are induced to participate by responding to challenges. If responses of silence (or, in cases such as Hare Krishna, with other techniques to frustrate deprogrammers, such as chanting) are met with by deprogrammers, further attempts to induce debate may be made. Violence, as illustrated in the following section, has at times been one such tactic.

VIOLENCE INVOLVED

Aside from the struggles of the demon to remain in possession of his victim, and the accompanying physical manifestations of this in the latter's body (sensationally depicted in the recent movie, *The Exorcist*), Robbins (1974: 215) mentions that flagellation of the possessed in medieval times was a common practice. Its purpose was "more to scorn the devil than afflict the demoniac." Restraint of the possessed, cruel by modern standards, was also common.

Similarly, verbal abuse targeted at the cult believer, his beliefs, and cult leaders is a fundamental tactic of deprogramming (see Rasmussen, 1976: 113). By relentless scatological discrediting of the cult, its awe and sanctity may be weakened. In addition, there are indications of physical, rather than just verbal, violence in deprogramming. The following is part of a transcript taken verbatim from a recorded interview with an anticult leader:

> Leader: It's [deprogramming] a bad thing to go through, because when it's your own child it nearly kills you. You think they're going to ruin your child. They [the child] may commit suicide or you don't know what. It's a horrible thing.
>
> Interviewer: Are the parents usually there at the deprogramming?
>
> Leader: They ought to be. If they're not, it gets out of hand . . . it becomes physical. You're encouraged to be there. I always urge people, if they're going to have a deprogramming, to be there. In the beginning they did it physically. They'd pick a guy up and throw him down if he wouldn't talk. [They'd say] 'You answer! You talk, damn you! You say something!' It was like a gang. They might slap him. It was the only way they knew . . . but it was very successful. That's all changed, but you still have too much physical abuse. Particularly when you have somebody who doesn't know or understand what they're doing, somebody who has just come out, full of hate for the cult and knowing they have to save the kid by making him forcefully listen. You have to force somebody to listen.

ALTERNATING THREATS AND APPEALS

According to Robbins (1974: 209ff.), alternating prayers and threats or exorcisms can produce a powerful psychological effect on the possessed person. An inspection of his abstract of the *Rituale Romanum,* a seventeenth-century rite of exorcism reprinted in 1947 by the New York Catholic diocese, shows three identical threat/appeal sequences. Each sequence is composed of a psalm reading, a prayer to God for divine aid during the rite, a Gospel Reading, another prayer, then the exorcism (a venomous disparagement of the possessing demon, including abusive name-calling, threats, and commandments to leave), followed finally by a prayer. After this sequence had been performed three times, the rite could be administered again as many times as necessary.

Bible-reading, particularly of sections from the New Testament that refer to false messiahs, such as the twenty-fourth chapter of Matthew, is an integral part of many deprogrammings. This constrasts with the violence already described. Patrick rarely went into a session without his Bible (Patrick and Dulack, 1976), and West (1975: 3) advocates readings of the scriptures interspersed through the process.

DEPROGRAMMING AS RESOCIALIZATION

The implicit reasoning involved in denying cult believers belief legitimacy seems to reduce to the following: (1) my (son, daughter, family member) has embraced a "strange" religion; (2) only inherently "strange" people would be voluntarily attracted to such a religion; (3) my (son, daughter, family member) is obviously not an inherently "strange" person; (4) hence, he or she must have been hoodwinked or brainwashed into participating. The "seduction premise," as Toch (1965: 226) calls it, is a familiar one in the rationales for persecution of social movements.[9] Through its logic, anticultists can deny that deprogramming represents counterbrainwashing or any violation of civil rights to freely select one's religion.

What, then, is deprogramming? The definition of resocialization offered by Kennedy and Kerber (1973: 39) could easily serve for deprogramming:

> Resocialization is that process wherein an individual, defined as inadequate according to the norms of a dominant institution(s), is subjected to a dynamic program of behavior intervention aimed at instilling and/or rejuvenating those values, attitudes, and abilities which would allow him to function according to the norms of said dominant institution(s).

Moreover, whatever its stated rationale, deprogramming bears a close resemblance to accounts of brainwashing, or radical resocialization. Richardson, Harder, and Simmonds

(1972) applied an 11-step model of brainwashing developed by Lifton (1963, 1957) to the "thought reform" of the Jesus movement and found, despite points of inadequacy, overall resemblance. This model involved, first, a "stripping process" designed to confuse the individual's assumptions of reality and identity with a reference group; second, a rechanneling of identification that leads the person to a new integration with a new (or former) reference group by way of a confession of past "errors"; and, finally, an ultimate "rebirth" of the self-concept safely ensconced within the approved limits of the new referents.[10] One crucial difference between Lifton's model and the conversion processes of marginal religions is the coercion factor. While there are few if any reported instances (not based on deprogrammed reiteration) of marginal religions gaining adherents by abducting and forcibly restraining them during proselytization, such coercion runs rampant throughout accounts of deprogramming. Based on current sociological understanding of the religious conversion process, the tendency of the probable convert to seek a religious solution to his or her problems is an essential predisposing factor (Lofland and Stark, 1965). This seems likely in the case of conversions to marginal religions. Nobody, however, ever claimed for the deprogrammees a predisposition to become deprogrammed.

CONCLUDING REMARKS

Possession and exorcism, rather than representing historically curious but extinct phenomena, are still with us. As two specific forms of more generic reactions to religious deviance, they are now labeled "psychological enslavement" and "deprogramming." In the 1970s, the rationale undergirding this pair of concepts has permitted families and friends of cult members to disenfranchize the legitimacy of the latter's religious commitment. This, in turn, may have significant implications for the future of religious freedom in this country. Meanwhile, it is ironic that while modern anticultists perceive commitment to cults' doctrines as the result of brainwashing, their own attempts to restore their loved ones to "normality" closely resemble the very phenomena they profess to despise.

A number of issues here, such as science's willingness to help define religious "legitimacy" from "illegitimacy," have been given only cursory attention and deserve further study. In particular, the historical definition of evil, and how to deal with it, requires development and integration into deviance theory. It is safe to make one generalization, however: Lifton's religious "totalism" (1963: 419), particularly those elements which he refers to as excessive conviction, is not the preserve of the religiously marginal.

NOTES

1. During the same month, 43 congressmen and one senator petitioned the new U.S. Attorney General, Griffin Bell, to investigate charges of "brainwashing," "mind control," and "mental manipulation" brought against certain religious groups (Conlan, 1977). The Justice Department demurred on the grounds that no clear violation of federal law, such as kidnapping or slavery, was demonstrated.

2. Since the anticult movement is in a current state of flux, with local ad hoc groups arising (some of which affiliate with the organizations listed below or become independent bodies) and others merging or dissolving, it is virtually impossible to present an exhaustive list of all such groups. However, it may be confidently stated that the following sample represents the more established and ideologically typical anticult organizations: The Citizens' Freedom Foundation (CFF); Return to Personal Choice, Inc.; The Spiritual Counterfeits Project (recently merged with the Berkeley Christian Coalition); Love Our Children, Inc.; Committee of the Third Day; Citizens Engaged in Reuniting Families, Inc. (CERF); The Individual Freedom Foundation (IFF); Citizens Organized for Public Awareness of Cults; Free Minds, Inc.; The International Foundation for Individual Freedom (IFIF); and the National Ad Hoc Committee Engaged in Freeing Minds (CEFM). Until recently, the last organization was the interim national coordinating committee for all groups. However, on March 1, 1977, these groups formed a coalition called the International Foundation for Individual Freedom (not the IFIF listed above). Its purposes are to raise funds, to disseminate information on cults to families and to the media, to lobby for anticult legislation, and to perform more effectively those functions with which local and national groups had been previously burdened.

3. The National Ad Hoc Committee Engaged in Freeing Minds (CEFM), located in Grand Prairie, Texas. See Shupe, Spielmann, and Stigall (1977) for a more detailed description of its purposes, operations, and functions.

4. For example, The Children of God have been accused of screening mail, deliberately deploying members to the opposite end of the country (or even abroad) away from their families, and maintaining nomadic evasion patterns, all to discourage family contacts (State of New York, 1975). Similar claims have been made against Hare Krishna and the Unification Church.

5. In one related study (Shupe et al., 1977), it was found that persons who possessed higher occupational prestige (physicians, university professors, and similar professionals) or material resources tended to predominate in initial anticult reactions directed toward such groups as Sun Myung Moon's Unification Church. This suggests that socioeconomic

status may be an important discriminator of families or individuals who remain active in the anticult movement after the initial goals of participation have been accomplished.

6. We encountered occasional allegations from anticultists concerning the use of drugs and latent or overt sexuality in cult membership recruitment.

7. It is not our purpose to dispute these claims, though there is mixed evidence as to whether the indoctrination methods used by marginal religious groups resemble the Korean War-style brainwashing. Journalistic accounts of the conversion process operating among many Unification Church missionary units (Rice, 1976; Rasmussen, 1976) indicate a gradual process of closure among religiously predisposed persons, rather than any sudden mind-numbing operation (for the importance of this predispositional factor, see Lofland and Stark, 1965). However, Richardson, Harder, and Simmonds (1972) applied an 11-step model of "thought reform" by Lifton (1963, 1957) to the Jesus movement when it possessed marginal status and found some similarities.

8. This view contrasts with evidence that such cults do in fact witness defections of conscious, disgruntled members. Of the dwindling membership base of the Unification Church, for example, Welles (1976: 38) states: "The church is now constantly losing members. While the arduous deprogramming often necessary to wrest devout Moon converts from the Divine Principle has gotten much publicity, many Moonies simply walk away from the church because they are worn out by the Spartan routine and frustrated and dispirited by the church's obsession with private gain instead of public betterment." The possession hypothesis was also contradicted, at least implicitly, in one of our interviews with the leader of a national-level anticult committee, when he admitted that there was likely some self-selection in the angry ex-cultists with whom he came in contact.

9. Toch (1965: 224) cites a similar instance of defining away a religion's legitimacy qua religion: "King Hussan II of Morocco . . . was questioned during a recent visit to New York about the impending execution in his country of three leaders of the Bahai sect, a social movement which preaches brotherhood and rationality. His Majesty responded that 'Islam was the state religion of Morocco but that there was freedom to all, to Christianity, Judaism, and Islam. "Bahai is not a religion, rather something that attacks public order." ' " See also Wallis (1975).

10. While it is not our intention to detail the social psychological processes occurring in this reconversion, readers will doubtlessly anticipate a number of alternative attitude change processes operating. For example, the cognitive dissonance perspective (Festinger, 1957) would emphasize the incongruous cognitions between relatives' positive self-images and the facts of their kin's cultic activities (as extensions of themselves), which lead to a redefinition of the marginal religious commitment's legitimacy. Attribution theory (Shaver, 1975; Bem, 1967a, 1967b, 1966) would focus on the deprogrammer's attempt to place the locus of marginal religious commitment on the manipulative external agencies, absolving the deprogrammee of responsibility for cult participation and facilitating reintegration into conventional society. In addition, Garfinkel's (1973) description of "degredation ceremonies" could also be applied to deprogrammers' attempts to disparage the cult status and replace it with one more acceptable to conventional society.

REFERENCES

BAUER, R. (1957) "Brainwashing: psychology or demonology?" J. of Social Issues 13: 41-47.

BEDNARSKI, J. (1970) "The Salem witch-scare viewed sociologically," pp. 151-163 in M. Marwick (ed.) Witchcraft and Sorcery. Baltimore, MD: Penguin.

BEM, D. (1967a) "An experimental analysis of self-perception," pp. 444-456 in M. Fishbein (ed.) Readings in Attitude Theory and Measurement. New York: John Wiley.

——— (1967b) "Self-perception: an alternative interpretation of cognitive dissonance phenomena." Psych. Rev. 74: 183-200.

——— (1966) "Inducing beliefs in false confessions." J. of Personality and Social Psychology 3: 707-710.

BIDERMAN, A. and H. ZIMMER [eds.] (1961) The Manipulation of Human Behavior. New York: John Wiley.

CARDOZO, A. (1970) "A modern American witch-craze," pp. 367-377 in M. Marwick (ed.) Witchcraft and Sorcery. Baltimore, MD: Penguin.

CFF (1974-1976) Citizens Freedom Foundation "News," Vols. I-III. Chula Vista, CA: Citizens Freedom Foundation.

CEFM [National Ad Hoc Committee Engaged in Freeing Minds] (1976) A Special Report, The Unification Church: Its Activities and Practices, Parts I and II. Arlington, TX: National Ad Hoc Committee, A Day of Affirmation and Protest.

CHALENOR, R. (1976) "Religion, mind control, money and power." Chula Vista, CA: Citizens Freedom Foundation. (pamphlet)

CLARK, J. (1976) "Investigating the effects of some religious cults on the health welfare of their converts." (Testimony of John G. Clark, Jr., M.D., to the Special Investigating Committee of the Vermont Senate.) Arlington, TX: National Ad Hoc Committee Engaged in Free Minds. (pamphlet)

CONLAN, M. (1977) "Officials ask probe of cult brainwashing." Fort Worth Star Telegram (February): 9a.

CRAMPTON, H. (n.d.) "Cult activities and youth involvement: money and power." Redondo Beach, CA: Volunteer Parents Chapter, Citizens Freedom Foundation. (pamphlet)

CRITTENDEN, A. (1976) "The incredible story of Ann Gordon and Reverend Sun Myung Moon." Good Housekeeping (October): 86, 90, 92, 94, 96, 98, 100.

FESTINGER, L. (1957) A Theory of Cognitive Dissonance. Stanford, CA: Stanford Univ. Press.

GARFINKEL, H. (1973) "Conditions of successful degradation ceremonies," pp. 53-60 in W. Filstead (ed.) An Introduction to Deviance. Chicago: Rand-McNally.

HUNTER, E. (1962) Brainwashing: From Pavlov to Powers. New York: The Bookmailer.

——— (1953) Brainwashing in Red China: The Calculated Destruction of Men's Minds. New York: Vanguard.

KELLER, E. (1974) "Glimpses of exorcism in religion," pp. 259-311 in St. E. Nauman, Jr. (ed.) Exorcism Through the Ages. New York: Philosophical Library.

KENNEDY, D. and A. KERBER (1973) Resocialization: An American Experiment. New York: Behavioral Publications.

KNICKERBOCKER, B. (1977) "Parents vs. religious cults." Christian Science Monitor (February): 9.

LIFTON, R. (1963) Thought Reform and the Psychology of Totalism. New York: W. W. Norton.

——— (1957) "Thought reform of Chinese intellectuals: a psychiatric evaluation." J. of Social Issues 13: 5-20.

LOFLAND, J. and R. STARK (1965) "Becoming a world-saver: a theory of conversion to a deviant perspective." Amer. Soc. Rev. 30 (December): 862-875.

MEERLOO, J. (1956) The Rape of the Mind. New York: World.

MERRITT, J. (1975) "Open letter." Lincoln, MA: Return to Personal Choice, Inc. (pamphlet)

MONTAGNO, M. (1977) "Is deprogramming legal?" Newsweek (February): 44.

OESTERREICH, T. (1974) "The genesis and extinction of possession," pp. 111-141 in St. E. Nauman, Jr. (ed.) Exorcism Through the Ages. New York: Philosophical Library.

PATRICK, T. and T. DULACK (1976) Let Our Children Go! New York: E. P. Dutton.

RASMUSSEN, M. (1976) "How Sun Myung Moon lures America's children." McCall's (September): 102, 104, 106, 108, 110, 112, 115-175.

RICE, B. (1976) "Honor thy father 'Moon'." Psychology Today 9 (January): 36-47.

RICHARDSON, J., M. HARDER, and R. SIMMONDS (1972) "Thought reform and the Jesus movement." Youth and Society 4 (December): 185-202.

ROBBINS, R. (1974) "Exorcism," pp. 201-216 in St. E. Nauman, Jr. (ed.) Exorcism Through the Ages. New York: Philosophical Library.

ROBBINS, T. (1977) "Even a Moonie has civil rights." The Nation (February 26): 238-242.

SARGENT, W. (1957) Battle for the Mind. New York: Doubleday.

SCHUPPIN, E. (n.d.) "Areas of government involvement in cults and pseudo-religious organizations." Arlington, TX: National Ad Hoc Committee Engaged in Freeing Minds. (reprinted pamphlet)

SHAVER, U. (1975) An Introduction to Attribution Processes. Cambridge, MA: Winthrop.

SHUPE, A., Jr., R. SPIELMANN, and S. STIGALL (1977) "Deprogramming and the emerging American anti-cult movement." Paper to be presented at the Annual Meeting of the Society for the Scientific Study of Religion, October.

SHUPE, A., Jr., J. VENTIMIGLIA, D. BROMLEY, and S. STIGALL (1977) "Political control of radically innovative religions." Paper presented at the Annual Meeting of the Society for the Scientific Study of Religion, Southwest, March.

STARKEY, M. (1961) The Devil in Massachusetts. New York: Dolphin.

State of New York (1975) "Final report on the activities of the Children of God to Hon. Louis J. Lefkowitz, Attorney General of the State of New York." Albany, NY: Charity Frauds Bureau.

TOCH, H. (1965) The Social Psychology of Social Movements. Indianapolis: Bobbs-Merrill.

TONER, P. (1974) "Exorcism and the Catholic faith," pp. 31-56 in St. E. Nauman (ed.) Exorcism Through the Ages. New York: Philosophical Library.

WALLIS, R. (1975) "Societal reaction to scientology: a study in the sociology of deviant religion," pp. 86-116 in R. Wallis (ed.) Sectarianism: Analyses of Religious and Non-religious Sects. London: Peter Owen.

WELLES, C. (1976) "The eclipse of Sun Myung Moon." New York Magazine (September 27): 33-38.

WEST, W. (1975) "In defense of deprogramming." Arlington, TX: International Foundation for Individual Freedom. (pamphlet)